John Wallace

port to port

port to port

Concept, Photography and Art Direction by Lisa Linder

L̲
B

Photography & Art Direction Lisa Linder

Design Studio Alta

Editor Susan Ward Davies

Production Coordinator Seonaid

Writers:
Oporto/The Douro Valley Karen Hampson

London Bryony Coleman

Venice Rob Ryan

Orient Express Jonathan Futrell

The Riviera Rebecca Fowler

Antwerp Jonathan Futrell

Ireland Seth Linder

New York Jennifer Jackson Alfano

First published 1996
Copyright © 1996 by Lisa Linder.
Photographs © 1996 Lisa Linder.

First published in the United Kingdom in 1996
by LB Publishing Ltd. Cedar House. 698 Green Lanes
Winchmore Hill, London N21 3RE.
ISBN 1 900942 00 3

Black and White printing by Melvin Cambettie Davies
at Master Mono.
Colour Origination by Radstock Reproductions,
Midsomer Norton.
Printed and bound in Great Britain by Butler and Tanner Ltd.

Special thanks to Neil, Sean and Craig.

Contents

Intro

Port wine originates from an area that is historically poor and hard working, but its principal following was, traditionally, the preserve of the upper class male who enjoyed it as an after-dinner drink with a fat cigar and a few good stories. But, as appreciation of international food and fine wine has grown, and tastes have become more sophisticated, Port wine, too, is experiencing a renaissance. It is being rediscovered, not just for its traditional digestive properties, but also as a drink for a new century, for a new generation.

In the past, travel was only for the very adventurous or the very privileged, but in the past few decades it has become more accessible for everyone, leading to a broader knowledge of - and interest in - other cultures. This global awareness has led to a familiarisation with food and drink from around the world, and, as a result, people have learnt to experiment. Instead of sticking rigidly to native traditions, we now draw on global inspiration in our ever more eclectic diets.

Sea ports have always been a breeding ground of change and innovation, places where travellers and traders would come together to exchange merchandise, news and ideas. As these ideas and customs spread from port to port, they are adapted and modified to suit each new environment. For this reason, we have focused on sea ports in our exploration of the rebirth of Port wine. On tracing the roots of its renaissance, we have followed some of the traditional trade routes from Oporto to those places - London, Venice, Antwerp, New York, Ireland and The Riviera - where its new image is already being formed. The story begins in the city of Oporto and in the Douro Valley, the birth place of Port wine.

Oporto

The *barcos rabelos* were the traditional means of bringing Port from the Douro Valley to Oporto

Oporto is the muse behind the name of the nation and of Port wine. Built on a series of hills at the mouth of the Douro river, the city is the workhorse of Europe's oldest nation state, formal, stately and industrious. An elegant combination of imposing granite buildings and the faded pastel houses down by the riverside, Oporto has always been a hub of commerce, and it is from here that Port begins its international journey. The pace is brisk and business-like, the people industrious and conservative. 'Coimbra studies, Braga prays, Lisbon plays and Oporto works,' is the old saying. The austere grey fabric of the city changes as it moves towards the river, where the medieval part of town has unexpected colour and charm. The narrow, cobbled streets are lined with tall houses which lean together for support and reach skywards, their wrought-iron balconies fluttering with washing.

The British have traded with Oporto since the 14th century and have been a permanent fixture in the city since the 18th. The Methuen Treaty of 1703 made the Douro Britain's main wine supplier and so the Port business was born. The English have put their own stamp on the city in the Port wine lodges lining the waterfront of Vila Nova de Gaia and The Factory House, a large, Palladian building on the cor-ner of Rua de Sao João and Rua do Infante Dom Henrique. Andre L. Simon, 19th century *bon viveur*, described it thus: 'The Factory House at Oporto is more than a wine exchange and social club; it is the Mecca for all Port lovers. Its granite house is spacious and cool; its twin dining rooms, ballroom and library have dignity and grace; their Chippendale furniture is exquisite; the glass, the silver and all furnishings are perfect; the cellar is simply wonderful.'

It was here, in 1809, that grateful Port wine mer-chants entertained the troops of Sir Arthur Wellesley (later Duke of Wellington) after he had driven Napoleon's troops out of Portugal for the second and last time. The Factory House remains, to this day, an exclusive club, membership still being confined to men in the Port wine business. Above this bastion of old-fashioned English taste, at the top of Penaventosa hill, stands Oporto's grand cathedral, the Se.

The magnificent stained glass windows of the Hotel Infante de Sagrès

Oporto bears more resemblance to a Northern European town than to its fellow cities in the South with their Mediterranean flavour. Small by contemporary standards, the city subsists on a diet of commerce. Edging the river across from the restaurants of the Ribeira are the lodges of the Port wine shippers. The terracotta roofs are splashed with their famous names: Sandeman, Taylors, Croft. The most instantly recognisable figure on the waterfront is the black-cloaked shape of the Sandeman Don, familiar to generations through successive advertising campaigns dating back to 1930. Founded in the city of London, in 1790, by George Sandeman, the Sandeman lodges have been housed in a former convent since 1813. Within the main office, believed to have been built by Joaquim da Costa Lima Sampaio,the same architect who built the British Factory House, is a museum illustrating the history of the company. Sandeman's reputation for commissioning innovative art work was established in 1926 with the controversy surrounding a poster by the French artist Jean d'Ylen. It is a beautiful piece of work in which a striking redhead is draped across the side of a centaur who holds two bottles of Sandeman's Port. This was well ahead of its time in recognising that sex sells, though not everyone in Britain was ready for it. A Mrs Smith of Leicester wrote:

'To say the least of it, I was thoroughly disgusted with the picture. The supposed man's expression is absolutely diabolical and lustful; the woman's pitiful and pleading. Is the woman to climb up the devil's back (excuse the expression) for a glass of wine? As a businesswoman, and one who likes a glass of Sandeman's within reason, I very much object to it.'

This prompted the response:

It seems there's a young lady from Leicester,
Who would not say no if you pressed her,
But the trollop who rides,
On the wild horse's sides,
Has put her off Port and depressed her.

Here, in 1387, an English Princess, Phillipa of Lancaster, married King João of Portugal. The original fortress-like Romanesque structure has been much embellished over the centuries, most flamboyantly by Nicolo Nazzoni, an Italian architect, who settled in Oporto and completely seduced her with his smooth, southern style. He was prolific. He dazzled with elaborate carvings and spirals with exuberant, baroque churches and palaces. He made the Duchess blush! Around Nazzoni, Oporto feels like a princess, albeit a portly one. As the city settles around the Douro, she casts a sideways glance at her reflection in the river and recognises herself as the capital of Portuguese baroque.

The people are industrious and conservative. 'Coimbra studies,

Braga prays, Lisbon plays and Oporto works', is the old saying

food in the region

To a surprising extent, the history of the area still determines its diet. Fresh fish is available around the coast, but not in the abundance that one might expect. Sardines can be found almost everywhere, as well as *bacalhau* (dried, salted cod), probably the most traditional dish in Portugal, both in the country and the seaside. The Portuguese, in fact, seem to have devised hundreds of recipes for its use, of which a good selection can be found on any of the local menus.

The Portuguese are very conservative, and any variation of their traditional cuisine is viewed with suspicion. This means that most restaurants have very similar menus. In Oporto, tripe is the most typical dish; also common are lamb and baby goat, and almost universally there is *caldo verde*, a cabbage and potato soup. Locally cured hams and cheeses are excellent, and the majority of desserts are deliciously sweet and sticky – made largely from egg yolks, sugar and almonds.

crème Queimado

1 tbsp plain flour
6 tbsp granulated sugar
1/2 litre milk
4 egg yolks
zest of a lemon cut into broad strips
2 small glasses of Sandeman Founder's Reserve Port
extra sugar for caramel

Serves 4

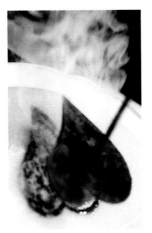

Put flour and sugar in a metal saucepan, gradually add a third of the milk, stirring continuously. Mix in egg yolks, add lemon zest, then stir in the rest of the milk. Place the pan on a medium heat and bring to the boil stirring continuously. The mixture will thicken when it boils. Continue stirring for 3 to 4 minutes, remove from heat and add Port. Pass the mixture through a sieve into a serving dish or dishes. Allow to cool.

Sprinkle surface of dish with a little granulated sugar and either brand the top with a hot iron, if you have one, or place under a very hot grill to caramelise the surface. Pour over a little Port, which will mix with the caramel to form a delicious sauce. Refrigerate for at least 1 hour before serving.

Recommended wine: Sandeman Founder's Reserve

Crème Brûlée
Angelina Queiroz Vides, Cook at Santa Clara, Sandeman's house in the Douro

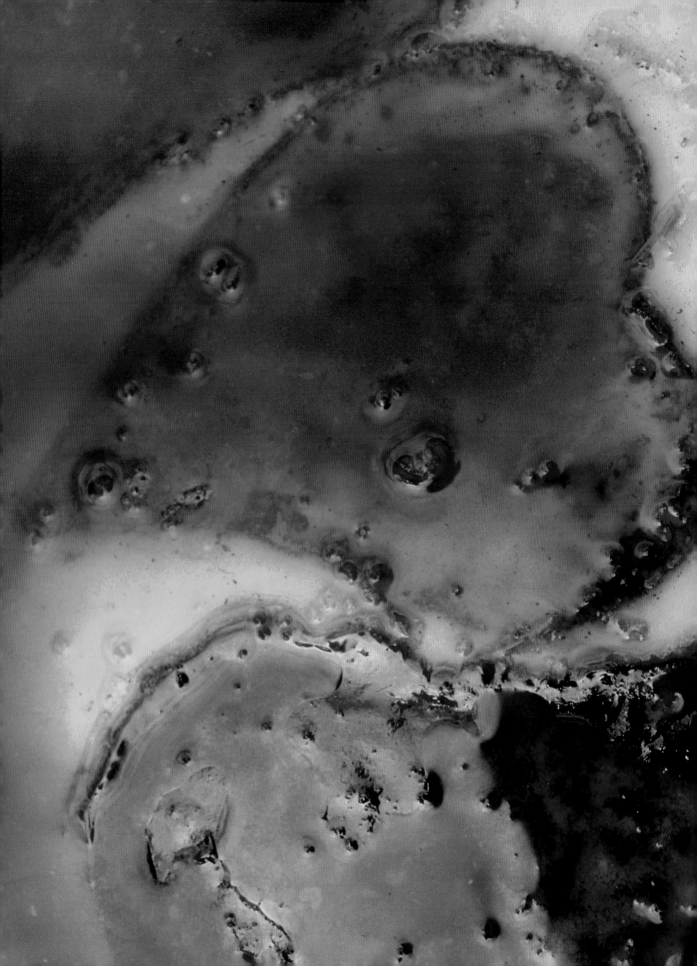

'For me, being able to produce here the best wine in the world is the only source of satisfaction. Port wine cannot be produced in flat, easy vineyards. I love the viticulture and the hard work. Here we engage in a fierce battle with the elements to produce top-quality wine with no help from God.'

Armando Almeida. Grape grower for Sandeman

The Douro Valley

To understand the nature of Port wine, it is necessary to travel 150 kms due east of Oporto, into the heart of the oldest demarcated wine-growing region in the world. Here, in a dramatically different landscape from Oporto, high in the Douro Valley, Port begins life in what have to be among the strangest and wildest vineyards in the world. Rock, precipice and gorge, the Douro Valley is a fortress with walls of up to 900 metres high. Here, tiny villages, stately *quintas* (farms) and small vineyards compete for space on steep slopes of granite and schist (a type of slate). The landscape is intricately ridged with terraces that look like a giant staircase to the top of the world.

The Douro river runs along the valley floor towards the Atlantic, thick, snake-like and sludgy green. The mountains rise spectacularly straight up from the river, and clinging to their steep, rocky sides, on man-made terraces, are the vines that will produce Port wine. The climate here is baking hot throughout the summer and freezing cold in winter. These are the vineyards of Hercules, steep, harsh and extremely labour-intensive, where neither beast nor machine can negotiate the inhospitable terrain. The majority of the great Port-producing *quintas* lie around or above the town of Pinhão. Armando Almeida owns Quinta de St Antonio in this area. He says: 'Here, there is no respite from anxiety until the wine is in the vat.' At the mercy of a series of micro-climates, the Douro Valley labours against freak weather patterns. In June 1993, a blizzard of hail hammered down on Quinta de St Antonio with disastrous effects. The violent storm lasted around 20 minutes and wiped out all 22 hectares of vine. It devastated the harvest and left Almeida with barely enough courage to continue. But, born and bred in this region, his heart is tied to the land: 'For me, being able to produce here the best wine in the world is the only source of satisfaction. Port wine cannot be produced in flat, easy vineyards. I love the viticulture and the hard work. Here, we engage in a fierce battle with the elements in order to produce top-quality wine, with no help from God.'

Previous page: view over the Pinhão Valley
Opposite: the Douro Valley

26

The landscape is intricately ridged with terraces
that look like a giant staircase to the top of the world

'Imagine these wines as twin infants:
I must assess the characteristics of each and then
decide how best they should be brought up.
One I send to live by the sea to have a
physical, outdoor life. The other I keep
in the city, spending much of his time indoors.
Tawnies and Rubies are like this.'

Carlos Silva, Master Blender for the House of Sandeman

With a sniff, gargle and a spit, Carlos Silva considers their potential and decides their future

In the Douro Valley there is an old viticultural adage: 'The poorer the soil, the better quality the grape'. Ground that is almost pure schist produces the best grapes, but in small amounts. Although the region has identified more than 100 different varieties, there are five types of grape that have been recommended as the best for the production of Port. The government, through the Port Wine Institute (IVP), limits each vineyard in the amount of Port it can produce each year, according to its individual characteristics and the needs of the market. Quality is the key to prosperity for the producers of the region. Of the 250,000 hectares which constitute the demarcated Douro wine-growing area, only 30,000 are under vine, and of the total wine produced each year, less than 50% will be allowed to be made into Port.

Harvesting begins when the grapes have achieved full ripeness, which is usually in the month of September. To make Port wine, the natural process of fermentation is stopped by the addition of neutral wine alcohol (brandy) which neutralises the work of the yeast before it turns all the grape sugar into alcohol. The union of the alcohol with the fermenting wine creates the Port, a naturally sweet, fortified wine. The newly-made Ports are then stored in big vats in the Douro, and are regularly assessed for characteristics and evolution.

As spring approaches, they await the call to Gaia which will come from the Master Blender. The vats are then checked and sealed for the journey. Gone now are the days of the *barcos rabelos*, the picturesque, Phoenician-style boats that for centuries carried the new vintage down to Gaia. Since the mighty river has been tamed by a series of dams, all Port wine has travelled by road.

Upon arrival in Vila Nova de Gaia, the wines are taken to the Sandeman Lodge and presented to the Head Blender, Carlos Silva, who has been refining his olfactory excellence with the company for more than 20 years. To produce Port wine he must combine the slow processes of nature with keen vigilance and expert knowledge. His job as head nose is that of the alchemist, under whose ever-watchful eye the big, bold wines of the Douro will undergo a fundamental transformation, emerging years later, complex, mature and sophisticated. From the beginning, the wines are under constant assessment. With a sniff, gargle and a spit, Mr Silva considers their potential and decides their future:

'Imagine these wines as twin infants: I must assess the characteristics of each and then decide how best they should be brought up. One I send to live by the sea to have a physical, outdoor life. The other I keep in the city, spending much of his time indoors. Tawnies and Rubies are like this. The Tawny ages in a small oak cask, where it can breathe and is in contact with the wood. In reacting with both air and oak, it develops physically. The Ruby stays sealed, first in large, stainless steel vats, then moving on to wooden storage casks. Less exposed, it retains its primary characteristics.'

Carlos Silva also decides which wines should be blended together so that each enhances the strength of the other. In this way, he layers subtle nuances of flavour and builds structure. Blending is the essence of Port wine, and in the nose of Carlos Silva lives the style of The House of Sandeman. Tradition, innovation and excellence are the qualities he must keep constantly in mind.

'These are the
and extremely
machine can

vineyards of Hercules, steep, harsh
labour-intensive, where neither beast nor
negotiate the inhospitable terrain.'

London

Since its debut in fashionable London society more than 300 years ago, Port has enjoyed an enduring reputation as the most distinguished of post-prandial drinks.

Traditionally quaffed in copious quantities by florid gentlemen as an aid to digestion and conversation, Port's popularity as 'the Englishman's wine' finds its roots in the deep hostilities between England and France at the turn of the 18th century, which led to blue-blooded patriots refusing to buy claret. Their allegiance switched comfortably to Port, the full, dark wine (sometimes known as 'blackstrap') from Portugal's Douro Valley, which was fortified with brandy to preserve it during its transportation to England. Satirist Jonathan Swift encapsulated the sentiments of his generation when he wrote:

Be sometimes to your country true,
Have once the public good in view.
Bravely despise Champagne at Court
And choose to dine at home with Port.

The advent of the French Revolution in 1789, and the subsequent war with Napoleon, only served to consolidate Port's popularity in England. To drink heavily and at length was the prevailing fashion amongst politicians, scholars and squires alike. The renowned man of letters, Dr Samuel Johnson, once boasted that: 'I have drunk three bottles of Port without being the worse for it. University College has witnessed this.'

Throughout the 18th century, Port would be drunk at the best tables during dinner, and well into the night, by gentlemen who could safely consume three or four bottles and remain upright. Their secret was to drink very slowly and out of very small glasses. One of the staunchest supporters of Port was William Pitt 'the Younger' (Prime Minister from 1783 -1801), who had been prescribed it as a boy to fortify his weak chest. He was reputed to start drinking Port at breakfast and to enjoy up to six pint bottles daily. Pitt's Whig opponents, four- and five-bottle men such as Charles James Fox (who often arrived in the Commons fit for nothing but his bed), and the dramatist, Richard Brinsley Sheridan, were said to be able to match Pitt glass for glass.

The 19th and 20th centuries have continued to see Port popular with academics and sportsmen alike. Dickens' novels abound with respectable Port drinkers such as Mr Pickwick and Mr Brownlow, while the novelist R S Surtees, witty documentor of country pursuits, has his merry Squire Jorrocks and Mr Sponge frequently partake of 'a good, strong, military Port.' There has even been a tendency among literary men to link the drinking of Port with great learning. Max Beerbohm called Port 'the milk of donhood', but Hilaire Belloc is more tongue-in-cheek in his *Lines to a Don*:

Dons admirable! Dons of Might
Uprising on my inward sight
Compact of ancient tales, and Port
And sleep – and learning of a sort.

It is thus that Port held its own as the superior after-dinner tipple until as recently as a decade ago, when an exaggerated wave of health-consciousness swept the capital. Briefly, Port languished, smeared by its traditional association with upper-class old men and fast, working-class girls. Yet, nowadays, even a passing acquaintance with London's more fashionable restaurants, bars and clubs suggests that Port is in vogue once more.

William Lebus of Bibendum Fine Wines describes Port as 'a gorgeous and seductive drink.' He explains that by using top-quality grapes, producers have risen to the challenge of creating a much lighter drink than traditional Port, and advises: 'Forget Vintage and Crusted; the future is LBV (Late Bottled Vintage) and some seriously sexy Tawnies.'

Serena Sutcliffe, Master of Wine and Director of Sotheby's Wine Department, adores her old vintage Ports, but is also known to enjoy a glass of white Port as a delicious summer drink, adding a slice of lemon and some mineral water to make a Port spritzer. Wine writer Andrew Jefford goes further, championing white Port as 'a heroic summer aperitif', adding: 'White Port is at its best drunk cold and neat, with salted almonds. Deep blue skies and lapping water are optional.' Port has most definitely come in from the cold.

davys

O plump head-waiter at The Cock,
To which I most resort,
How goes the time? 'Tis five o'clock.
Go fetch a pint of Port.
Alfred, Lord Tennyson
Will Waterproof's Lyrical Monologue

While Soho makes a big noise about its rekindled love affair with Port, City movers and shakers have never stopped quietly adoring it. Not for Davys ale- and Port-houses the lurid lighting and art-house effects of modern eateries. Showing a healthy disregard for Nineties' fashions, some 50 venues provide a backdrop for those who still crave for the trappings of a Dickensian Britain, promising sawdust, stone flagging, aged oak barrels and seasoned pewter. Now celebrating its 126th year, Davys is a family-run concern, and its hostelries capture the essence of old-fangled ways, with names such as The Boot and Flogger (the boot was a solid leather bottle holder; the flogger was used to smack the cork into the bottle), The Crusting Pipe and The Bishop of Norwich (named after the gentleman with the inexcusable habit of never passing the Port).

Her Port in bottles stood, a well-stain'd row,
Drawn for the evening from the pipe below...
George Crabbe
The Borough
(Describing the Queen Caroline Tavern)

At Davys, house Ports are served in copper jugs from hogsheads and pipes, and such is the demand that 16,000 bottles were consumed in 1994 alone, with Sandeman Vintages 1967, 1970 and 1980 proving particularly popular. Davys' cavernous cellars in Greenwich hold almost 14,000 bottles of unusual Vintage wines and Ports dating back to 1837, and even, it is said, wine acquired from Prime Minister Gladstone's cellars. Any Vintage may be decanted to order at a couple of days' notice, a Sandeman 1935, for example, which would set you back an eminently reasonable £115. Demand, says director James Davy, is great.

'Port is the other woman; it's not drunk very openly and it can keep you up too late. But I don't give a damn about traditions; the right way to pass a bottle is to pass it directly to me, wherever I'm sitting.' Jeffrey Bernard

Hard drinkers

'Squire Mytton, the great Regency eccentric and sportsman, was reputed to start his day with a glass of Port. In fact, it was said that he drank an entire bottle of it while he was shaving in the morning. He is probably best remembered as the man who set fire to himself to cure his hiccups, and possibly it was Port that sustained him sufficiently to be able to wrestle with a Russian bear he kept, after dinner parties. At Doncaster Races he once won £10,000 and fell asleep counting the bank notes in his coach on the way back to London. When he arrived he found that they had all blown out of the window. He remarked to his coachman, and so coined the phrase: 'Easy come, easy go.' He was once seen shooting ducks on a frozen lake in midwinter dressed only in a nightshirt, hopping from one foot to the other on the ice exclaiming, "Oh, can't I bear pain well. Can't I bear pain well." When he died, still a young man and in exile, he was mourned by the entire nation.'

© Jeffrey Bernard

Outraged at the suggestion that it causes hangovers, Auberon Waugh blames instead the mixing of drinks, and remembers holidays in the Douro where he has often happily 'enjoyed 15 or 16 glasses of Port in an evening and woken up feeling as frisky as a deer.'

Admirers of Squire Mytton would be hard pressed to find such hell-raising role models in the clean-living Nineties, yet there are a few Soho stalwarts who nobly strive to keep the old rituals of hard drinking and bad behaviour alive and in reasonably good shape. They can be located in more traditional venues such as Auberon Waugh's literary enclave, the Academy Club in Soho. Waugh, editor of *The Literary Review*, columnist of *The Daily Telegraph* and crusader against modern poetry, is convinced that Port has suffered some grave injustices. Outraged at the suggestion that it causes hangovers, he blames instead the mixing of drinks, and remembers holidays in the Douro where he has often happily 'enjoyed 15 or 16 glasses of Port in an evening and woken up feeling as frisky as a deer.'

Writer Jeffrey Bernard is one of the people who invented the 'Soho Scene' in the Fifties. Famous for his love of horses, women and the bottle, the excesses of Bernard's technicolour lifestyle have been immortalised by Keith Waterhouse in the play *Jeffrey Bernard is Unwell*, *The Spectator's* euphemistic excuse for the weeks in which Bernard was too tired and emotional to produce his *Low Life* column. Bernard, a self-confessed vodka-and-tonic man, has always had a soft spot for Port: 'It's not a drink you drink steadily all the time like vodka or whisky, but I've often had Port after a meal in restaurants, particularly with old cronies from *The Sunday Times*. I used to keep a little bit at one time, but I never swigged it. Port is the other woman; it's not drunk very openly and it can keep you up too late. But I don't give a damn about traditions; the right way to pass a bottle is to pass it directly to me, wherever I'm sitting.'

On the occasion of his 30th birthday, restaurateur and London club owner Tom Bantock, who had hitherto never touched a drop of alcohol, drank three bottles of Port. Since that happy occasion, he has continued to consume three bottles of Port every day, enjoying his first glass before he leaves his bed. In the late Eighties, Bantock ran the fashionable Andrew Edmunds restaurant in Soho in return for a free room above the bar and 3,276 bottles of Port. It was here that the Bantock Cocktail was invented — Port and Champagne in equal measures, which is 'not half as bad as it sounds.' Bantock, notorious for causing restaurants to run out of Port, went on to launch Blacks in 1992. Blacks is a very successful private club in Soho's Dean Street, which encourages female members, and sells a steady two or three bottles of Port a week to customers. Bantock himself consumes a further 21. He says: 'I have only twice had a Port drinking competition. I won the first (downing four pints in two minutes) and my adversary collapsed in the gutter. The second contest I lost, seven – six bottles to my opponent.'

'I always hold Cuba in my mouth.' Win
door to the vulgarities of life.' Franz
ment to an elegant lifestyle.' George
smoking what a great wine is to the art
ionable celebrities are always surround

Sotheby's

Tom Bantock's penchant for Port has led him to learn a great deal about the best ways of acquiring it.

'A good way to buy Vintage Port is at country auctions, particularly of the local-doctor-dies-house-contents-up-for-sale variety. I suspect that doctors and vets receive endless Christmas presents from their patients to keep them sweet. The estate of dead, rural, professional oddbods regularly includes items such as "Lot 344, four bottles of Port, labels illegible, what am I bid?" This is how I buy all my Vintage Port. If the label has rotted or worn to a state of illegibility the stuff's obviously old, and the only old Port anyone's likely to store is bound to be Vintage. But watch out, many a bottle of Vintage Port has had to be poured down the drain because it was stored upright and the air got in.'

Port has always featured in the cellars of great men, and Sotheby's, auctioneers since 1744, traditionally sold wine along with the contents of complete house sales. In 1970, due to demand, a specialised wine department was setup. Now there is a large wine sale in Bond Street each month, as well as auctions abroad and off-site sales direct from distinguished cellars. Vintage Port has always been a popular feature of these sales, and has proved a wise investment for many. Serena Sutcliffe, Master of Wine and Director of Sotheby's Wine Department, remarks: 'Young Vintages to lay down for future drinking are remarkably reasonable, while great, mature Vintages are less expensive than you might think.' Sutcliffe is a great champion of Port, and, being a true oenophile, she fearlessly fails to observe rituals: 'At Sotheby's lunches and dinners, we've abandoned a couple of traditions. Our sommelier pours the Port for our guests rather than letting them push it around the table themselves. It encourages women to drink it. We always decant Port, and use special glasses for both Vintage and Tawny Ports, which are similar to large, more elegant copitas. The traditional Port glass is minute and, because it is always filled to the brim, you don't get the pleasure of the bouquet because you can't swill the glass without spilling the Port.'

ston Churchill 'A good cigar closes the
Liszt 'Cigars are the perfect comple-
Sand 'A Havana cigar is to the art of
of drinking.' Alain Senderens 'Our fash-
ed by a cloud of smoke.' Jules Sandeau

Port & cigars

Simon Chase, Marketing Director of London-based cigar importers Hunters and Frankau, is passionate about his cigars and his Port: 'To observe the time-honoured ritual of Port and cigars properly, the Port should be Vintage and the cigars from Havana. Each shares a similar heritage, as was evidenced in 1990 when the houses of Sandeman and Hunters and Frankau both celebrated their bicentenaries.

'Matching the sweet, subtle flavours of a great Port Vintage to a Havana demands care. There is a suitable richness of taste in all the renowned Vuelta Abajo tobaccos used for Cuba's *grandes marques,* but you'd be well advised to choose from one of the fuller-flavoured Havana brands like Partagas, Bolivar, Ramon Allones or Cohiba in its fatter formats.

'The size of cigar depends mainly on the time you have to devote to it. The sight of a decanter would commend a Churchillian Partagas Lusitania or a Cohiba Esplendido, while the prospect of a modest glass would suggest something smaller like Bolivar's robusto-sized Royal Corona.

'Whichever brand or size you favour, you should take a cigar with a dark outside leaf. This adds a sweet top taste to its underlying flavour, which will blend with the succulence of the Port.

'A debate rages over the order in which the wine and the cigar should be consumed. Port buffs frown on those who light up before the palate has experienced the nuances of a fine Vintage, while the keenest cigar *aficionados* advocate that no Port or coffee should be touched until the whole Havana has been savoured.

'Make up your mind where your loyalties lie and act accordingly. No matter how hard this proves, don't dip your cigar in the Port. Even if the Port survives unadulterated, the cigars won't, as Havanas absorb the aromas which surround them. Let the glorious flavours meet in your mouth and nowhere else.'

Sir Terence Conran, design guru, is the founder of Habitat and The Conran Shop, and more recently proprietor of a clutch of fashionable London restaurants: Bibendum, Cantina del Ponte, Butler's Wharf Chop House, Quaglino's, Pont de la Tour and Mezzo.

'I was first introduced to Port and the life of the *bon viveur* by the world's greatest authority on Port, a man called Wog Delaforce,' says Conran. 'He used to take me to lunch at Wilton's, just off St James's, where we'd eat a lot of oysters and then enjoy a glass of Port. His knowledge of Port was absolutely monumental. Blind-tasting he could usually get the year and vineyard right, and he'd even discuss which part of the vineyard the Port came from. I'm very fortunate because I was born in 1931, a lousy year for every other wine, but the greatest year ever for Port, and people quite often give me bottles of Vintage 1931 for birthday presents. I've never smoked cigarettes, I loathe them, but I love cigars, and to me there's nothing more pleasurable than sitting in the garden at about eight o'clock with a

Sir Terence
glass of Vintage Port in one hand and a Hoyo
Conran
de Monterrey Epicure No. 2 Havana in the other, with no one around but a few pigeons fluttering and cooing in the tree-tops.'

Women & Port

Right: Mary-Lou Sturridge and Anna Hugo at 192

Evelyn Waugh wrote: 'Women still regard Port as their natural enemy,' and it is fair to say that historically Port has not been the favoured drink of fashionable girls. At a time when it was zealously and copiously enjoyed by the gentlemen, women were expected to partake only for medicinal or for dissolute purposes. More recently, Port (with *de rigueur* splash of lemonade) has been thought of as the vulgar tipple of working-class women, although the Queen Mother is said to enjoy a glass, as does a certain centenarian nun, who recently confessed in the national press to the daily fortification of a small glass of Port.

Yet some of London's most stylish women have rediscovered Port with a passion. Anna Hugo, the manager of 192, in Kensington Park Road, one of West London's most happening bar/restaurants, says: 'People drink Port all the time at 192, young and old, male and female. If anyone coming in is feeling a bit rough, we give them Port and brandy to buck them up. They usually end up drinking it for the rest of the evening. The kitchen also uses a huge amount of Port in the cooking. I send half a bottle down to the chef every day.'

Port's new popularity comes as no surprise to Hugo, who grew up drinking Port at home with her father, and has since converted many girlfriends. She recalls an occasion when, seven years ago, she was on holiday in Lisbon with a girlfriend. 'It rained all the time, and every night we'd get a copy of *The Independent* and sit in the Port Wine Institute doing the crossword and sampling delicious Ports. Today, I frequently drink white Port as an aperitif, and often keep a bottle in the fridge. And I love Ruby Port with a piece of cake at tea-time. Sometimes, if there's a big group of us out for the evening, we might order a bottle of Vintage Port.'

Mary-Lou Sturridge is the popular general manager of the most celebrated members-only club in Soho, The Groucho Club, and probably knows more about who's in, who's out and who's under the table than anyone else in London. When she's not running The Groucho Club (named after Groucho Marx who said he would never belong to any club that would accept him as a member), she's fronting her Country & Western band *The Country Gentlemen*, belting out Patsy Cline numbers before an appreciative audience at venues such as The Atlantic Bar and Grill. 'Sometimes I drink Port before a show to loosen my vocal chords, or when my throat feels a bit tight,' she says. 'I grew up with six brothers and sisters, and we all used to drink Port at home. I adore Vintage Port after a great dinner, and if it's a good bottle, I always decant it, but I don't bother much with the other customs. My parents still tell me off for forgetting to pass the Port to my left. I think I have only once been asked with the other women at the table to leave the room after dinner. We went, but we took the Port decanter with us.'

Atlantic Cocktail

**Shake together a shot of brandy,
a shot of Sandeman Ruby Port and two
teaspoons of crème de mûre, then
pour over crushed ice
and serve with a black cherry.**

Oliver Peyton's phenomenally successful
restaurant, The Atlantic Bar and Grill,
lends itself as a natural barometer of
London's social climate. Since its
opening, in April 1994, it has quickly
established itself as a playground for
some of Soho's more stylish characters.
It is here, amidst the vast, lavish,
contemporary art deco-esque interior,
that we find the stirrings of Port's
renaissance as a drink for London's
gilded youth. The crowd at Peyton's
place drink what they like, not what they
think they should like, which is why
Port is back in vogue.
The Atlantic's original head barman,
Dick Bradsell, who now presides over
his own establishment, Detroit, has
even created two seriously smart Port-
based cocktails, namely the eponymous
Atlantic Cocktail and the more
traditional New Orleans Punch.

New Orleans Punch

**Shake together one and a half shots of
Sandeman LBV (Late Bottled Vintage)
Port, one and a half shots of brandy,
one shot of lemon juice, two teaspoons
of sugar syrup and two shots of
orange juice. Put ice cubes in a tall
glass, and pour in the mixture.
Top with soda or cold tea and decorate
with slices of orange and lemon.**

Pears poached in port wine and spices

4 firm pears
1/3 bottle of Sandeman Ruby Port
500g caster sugar
2 cinnamon sticks
6 cloves
1 large piece of root ginger
zest of 1 lemon and 1 orange
3 sprigs of thyme

Serves 4

Peel pears and place in a bowl, covering them with citrus juices. In a heavy-bottom pan, place all the other ingredients, excluding the Port, along with 570 mls of water, bring to boil and simmer for 15 minutes.
Add the Port and simmer for a further 5 minutes.
Place pears in this syrup, cover with a sheet of greaseproof paper and a plate to keep the pears submerged, and withdraw from the heat.
Leave the pears in the syrup until softened (test first with a knife). Remove from the pan and leave refrigerated overnight in the syrup.

Place the pears in a bowl with a little of the syrup and then cover with crushed Amaretto biscuits and crème fraîche.

Recommended wine: Sandeman Ruby Port

Alastair Little
Chef/Proprietor Alastair Little restaurant

12 chicken livers
1/2 cup of good smoked bacon cut into lardons
salt and freshly ground black pepper
Salad: mixture of fine salad leaves:
1/2 rosso
1/2 radicchio
1/2 frisée
olive oil
balsamic vinegar

Sauce:
2 large shallots
2 cloves garlic
2 large glasses of Sandeman Port (Ruby orTawny)
1 cup of good brown chicken stock
1 tbsp unsalted butter

Garnish:
stale bread for croutons
chives

Serves 4

Salad of chicken livers and bacon with port wine sauce

For the sauce: Sweat off chopped shallots and garlic in a little oil until softened, add the Port wine and reduce by half to two thirds. Add the chicken stock and bring to the boil. Add the butter and whisk until dispersed. Remove from heat.

For the salad: Add a few dashes of balsamic vinegar to 3 tbsp of olive oil and salt and pepper in a bowl and toss your salad leaves in it. Add croutons.

To finish: Take a hot pan with a little oil, fry bacon until it becomes crisp, add seasoned livers and cook on both sides for 2-3 minutes.

Divide salad between 4 plates, place livers and bacon on top; pour sauce over and garnish with chopped chives.

Recommended wine: Rioja, such as
Vina Ardanza Riserva

Alastair Little
Chef/Proprietor, Alastair Little restaurant

Crème d'oignons au porto

550g onions, finely chopped
65g unsalted butter
75g fennel, finely chopped
75g leeks, chopped
1 litre chicken stock
100ml double cream
50ml Sandeman Ruby Port
salt and pepper

Serves 4

Place onion and butter in saucepan and sweat until transparent. Add the chopped fennel, leeks, chicken stock, salt and pepper and simmer slowly for about 25 minutes until all ingredients are well cooked. Liquidise and pass through a fine sieve. Return soup to heat and stir in the double cream. Add the Port and season to taste. Ladle the soup into bowls and garnish with a spoonful of Port.

Recommended wine: Pouilly Fumé
(A Dézat) 1994

Anton Edelmann
Maître Chef de Cuisine, The Savoy

Chef's choice

London's top restaurateurs select their favourite combinations of Port and food

Le Gavroche

43 Upper Brook Street, London W1,
tel 0171 408 0881

MICHEL ROUX (Chef Proprietor): 'The last time I drank White Port was with a lobster dish. As a substitute for sherry, it's good with game soup or game terrine. Red Port is a little more difficult to match with food because of its strength, but it's delicious with chocolate puddings, so I suggest serving Ruby Port with my Gourmandise aux Trois Chocolats. Of course, a good Vintage Port is perfect with blue cheese. I adore Vintage Port, but I don't drink it too often because I like to drink good Port in quantities. I can do a bottle on my own, no problem.'

The Brackenbury

129-131 Brackenbury Road, London W6,
tel 0181 748 0107

ADAM ROBINSON (Chef Proprietor): 'I love Port, particularly a good Vintage after a good dinner, but you could drink Port throughout a meal; perhaps White Port with my Chilled Duck and Beetroot Consommé; and Ruby Port with Venison Terrine, while Vintage Port is very good with fresh cob nuts and unpasteurised Cashel Blue cheese.'

Dell'Ugo

56 Frith Street, London W1,
tel 0171 734 8300

ANTONY WORRALL THOMPSON (Chef Proprietor of some 21 restaurants, including The Atrium, 190 Queen's Gate and Drones): 'White Port is a delicious cold aperitif, and I love it in that boring old dish Port and melon, preferably a chilled Charentais. I've used Ruby Port in marinades often, but I would rather serve Tawny Port to accompany food such as a fairly strong double consommé, for example, oxtail consommé. A deep, red Vintage would go well with a strong cheese such as Stilton, or a Christmassy-type pudding such as my Open Mincemeat Tart.'

Leith's

92 Kensington Park Road, London W11,
tel 0171 229 4481

NICK TARYAN (Managing Director): 'The Sandeman 20-Year-Old Tawny has, especially when chilled, a crispness and acidity underlined by a sweetness which blends with the same qualities in a cold fruit or vegetable-based starter. Chef Alex Floyd's Pressed Baby Leeks with Langoustine, Scallops, Cured Salmon and Olive Oil displays that sweetness, whilst the addition of fish balances the flavours. The power of this Tawny will still show through, as will that of the fish. I would match Sandeman Partners' Ruby Port with Warm Chocolate Tart with Vanilla Ice Cream and a Compote of Cherries. The key to this match lies in relative richness. Richness and sweetness are often confused. The Chocolate Tart certainly has sweetness, but also has a richness and even a little tannin and bitterness from the cocoa which reflects the qualities of Sandeman Partners' Ruby Port with its rich weight of fruit and subtle tannins.
'The traditional perception of Port and cheese can be borne out by the fine combination of Sandeman Signature Port and a selection of traditional and new British cheeses. The old-fashioned idea that the cheese has to be Stilton can be rather misguided – the blue in any cheese is raw protein which counteracts tannin and will knock the balance of all but the most tannic of wines. Here the characteristic of age and added complexity in Sandeman's exceptional new Signature Vintage Character Port complements some of the more subtle flavours in the cheeses.'

Kensington Place

210 Kensington Church Street, London W8,
tel 0171 727 3184

ROWLEY LEIGH (Chef/Partner): 'I'd serve White Port with Beef Consommé with Melon, Ruby Port with Sun-Dried Raisin Cake with Crème Fraîche, and Vintage Port with a really good mature cheddar, such as Montgomery's, and Bath Olivers.'

Vong

Wilton Place, London SW1,
tel 0171 235 1010

TOM DIMARZO (Chef): 'White Port is good with Lobster with Thai Herbs because the Port brings out the sweetness in the lobster and serves as a contrast to the tartness of the white sauce. Ruby Port is full of body and goes well with Spiced Rack of Lamb and Exotic Spices. Tawny Port enhances the woody flavour of the mushrooms in Sea Bass in Sweet and Sour Mushroom Broth, and Vintage Port complements the gamey and coppery flavour of squab in Crispy Squab on Egg Noodle Pancakes with Honey Ginger Glazed Pearl Onions.'

Pied à Terre

34 Charlotte street, London, W1,
tel 0171 636 11778

BRUNO ASSELIN (Sommelier): 'I would serve a chilled White Port with creamy soups, perhaps with white mushrooms and also with poached oysters. For example we serve Asparagus Cappuccino Soup with Oyster Mushrooms and Scallops. Ruby Port I would recommend with our Chocolate Soufflé. Tawny Ports complement blue cheese and Stilton, and I would also serve it with woodcock, snipe, grouse, quail and pigeon. At Pied à Tierre, we would recommend Tawny Port with our Boned Pigeon, Roasted Garlic and Honey Sauce or Pigeon Breast and Confit Pâté with Celeriac Fondant.'

Les Saveurs

37a Curzon Street, London W1,
tel 0171 491 8919

JOEL ANTUNES (Chef): 'The French drink Port as an aperitif and will often have a Ruby or young Tawny Port before a meal. Port goes well with meats, particularly game. Serve a 10-Year-Old Tawny Port with Foie Gras aux Epices Orientales et Pruneaux (Foie gras with Oriental Spices and Prunes); serve a young Vintage Port – 1983 or 1985 – with Canard à l'abricot et Compote de Figues (duck with apricot and a compote of figs); serve a 1970 Vintage Port with Assiette de Fromages Bleues, Fourme d'Ambert, Bleu d'Aubergne, avec Poire, et Pain Pruneaux et Cerise (blue cheese with pear, prune and cherry bread. All the above should be served at 18°C. Finally, serve 10-Year-Old

Tawny Port at cellar temperature (12°/c) with Multicolore de Melon au Basilic, Caramel au Port' (mixed melons with basil and a port caramel).

Coast

26b Albemarle St, London W1,
tel 0171 495 5999

STEPHEN TERRY (Chef): 'You could drink chilled White Port with a Vinaigrette of Confit Chicken, Grilled Asparagus and Roasted Sweetbreads Engelée, which is served cold. I could easily drink Ruby Port with Roast Sea Bass on a Croute of Herbed Risotto, Grilled Venteche with a Piquante Velouté Sauce, because the sauce already contains very reduced red wine and Port. And Vintage Port could complement a couple of my puddings: Soup of Summer Fruits with Fromage Blanc, or Sweet Confit of Tomatoes with Vanilla Cream.'

Rules

35 Maiden Lane, London WC2,
tel 0171 497 1081

NEIL PASS (Chef): 'White Port is good chilled, as the delicate flavour is refreshing when served with starters, such as Mussels with Saffron and Parsley. Tawny Port is a wonderful accompaniment to all our game dishes as the smoothness of the Tawny complements the robust flavour of the meat. Ruby, on the other hand, enhances the flavour of any meat dish such as our Ox Cheek with Parsnip Purée. We serve half a Stilton at the table with our Vintage Port as the smooth creamy flavour is the perfect combination.'

The Four Seasons

Hamilton Place, Park Lane, London W1,
tel 0171 499 0888

ERICK BECQUEMONT (Chef Sommelier):
'Drier White Ports are good as an aperitif and should be served like sherry. Play with acidity and serve appetisers or canapés which are acidity based, for example, tomatoes, as these will complement White Ports and stimulate the appetite. Ruby Port is fun: for my adventurous clients I recommend it with a light chocolate dessert. This works because of the sugar content of Ruby Port which has a cocoa taste. Vintage Port comes after a meal or with cheese, as is the tradition.'

Venice

Start as you will definitely go on in Venice, even if you don't mean to, by spending more money than is entirely necessary. The approach from Marco Polo airport to Venice is the finest arrival in any city in Europe, possibly the world. Do you really want to see it peering through the salt-encrusted, scratched windows of a slow, public *motoscafo*? Hire a water taxi instead, and let an insouciant, Ray Ban-ed Master of the Waterways power you between the *bricole*, the bunches of wooden stakes that mark the safe passage towards that strange blur in the distance.

This way, you can stand on deck and watch the watery mirage sharpen into bricks and mortar rising miraculously from the murk of the lagoon. As the throttle is opened to hurtle you closer, the multiplicity of towers and domes that make up this archipelago becomes apparent, and as you pass by your first island, you can pick out buildings streaked with pigments from the palettes of Bellini, Carpaccio, Titian or Tintoretto. Venice is at the same time un-believably magical and utterly ridiculous, two reactions that are going to jostle for your attention the whole time you are in the city.

The ridiculousness comes to the fore almost immediately, not only in the size of your aqua-cabbie's bill (close enough to £40 to give it a firm handshake), but also as he steers you down some minor canal, almost brushing the peeling, bruised walls of faded burnt sienna, along his equivalent of a rat-run to the Grand Canal. That is when you first wonder

if you are ever going to make sense of this mad, aqueous maze.

Many people will tell you that your first action should be to head straight for the great galleries of Venice, the Accademia or the Guggenheim, or the Doge's Palace. But that isn't going to get you your bearings. I would say spend your time first of all looking at, and trying to understand, the greatest work of art of all - Venice itself.

This medieval masterpiece is a complex tapestry of 117 islands - some claim 118 - separated by more than 100 canals and stitched together by 400 bridges. The fine threads that run over this background are the *calli*, the thousand of tiny alleys that twist and turn and mislead, bursting on to squares, diverting around churches and canals, inevitably depositing you in some spooky, echoing, drip-drip-dripping dead end.

Don't worry - getting lost in Venice is part of its charm, and although you may think you will never find your way home, sooner or later you will find a sign you want to kiss with relief - *Per Rialto* it will say, directing you to the famous bridge, or *Per San Marco*, your salvation pointing to one of the greatest squares in Europe, dominated by the Doge's Palace, St Mark's Basilica and the Campanile tower. (Most of Venice is the unreconstituted genuine article - the tower is, strictly speaking a replica, the original having played house-of-cards on July 14, 1902.) The Piazza San Marco will form the hub of your visit, the place

where you catch the *vaporetti* (from the Piazzetta dock), stroll in the evening or loiter at midday, calculating whether you can afford yet another coffee at Florian. It will be your zero meridian, from which all other Venetian destinations will be measured, for the entire trip.

But before you risk taking to the alleys, jump a *vaporetto* and get orientated. The classic first-time ride is line 34, caught from San Marco, which will take you past two and a half miles of exquisite palaces and bridges, with views recognisable, and unchanged, from Canaletto, Francesco Guardi and Luca Carlevaris, Turner and Renoir. It is along here, as you head up the Grand Canal, that you first become aware of the true scale of the folly of Venice - a whole city moving about on water. Police launches and ambulances roar by, bricks destined to shore up some crumbling edifice are being unloaded, great mounds of fruit and vegetables are transported to and from the Rialto market, taxis zip by, narrowly missing the *traghetti - gondolas* used to cross canals (not to be confused with the tourist version - for a start, you stand in a *traghetto*, secondly, they are dirt-cheap compared with the hustling *gondoliers*). This, you realise, is the original – and even more daring and extravagant – *Waterworld*.

Then take line 5, the *circolare*, which runs either *sinistra* or *destra* - left or right - circumnavigating the core of Venice and over to San Michele and across to the glass-blowing island of Murano (where glass is actually no cheaper, and may even be dearer than back in the shops you have just left), making it the best city tour in town. But the other advantage of line 5 is that it passes through the Arsenale, where Venice's mastery of shipbuilding was refined, but which is now off-limits except to the *vaporetto*. The giant barracks, basins and workshops are dumb testimony to the sheer power of old Venice in the centuries when it dominated the eastern trade routes. The Arsenale is eerie and awesome - 700 years of sea power moth-balled until the mythical

'Sooner or later every visitor seems to pass through the doors of Harry's Bar.'

time when the city rises again. As you pass out of the complex back on to the Grand Canal, turn around and look at the triumphalist gate, built by Antonio Gambello in 1460, from a drawing by Jacopo Bellini. It is bracketed by a pride of lions, liberated from their original sites in Greece.

By now, deposited back at San Marco, you will be hungry and thirsty, and the chances are your thoughts will turn to the other kind of Bellini, the sparkling Prosecco-and-peach variety served up at Harry's Bar, which is but a few steps from the Piazza. Physically, the bar, all primrose and wood panels, is dwarfed by its reputation as one of the great bars of the world - it is, in fact, surprisingly cosy. However – and this is probably a Venetian heresy – I would skip a Bellini. They are overrated, overpriced and mass-produced. There is none of the flair and magic I associate with great cocktail-making – this is such a production line, you almost expect a McDonald's-type boast: 'Over 10 million served'. So how about a Port? There is certainly some kept behind that famed mahogany bar. It will raise an eyebrow or two, certainly, although our waiter recovered his poise admirably: 'Ah, life is bitter. We need something sweet from time to time.' Well, your Port will be a talking point, that's for sure. Not that you need one in Harry's: sooner or later, every visitor seems to pass through those doors, only too keen to share their Venetian experiences with you. That is why it is one of the greatest watering-holes, and why one drink – of any hue – inevitably turns into four.

But Harry's is not the only game in town. You are more likely to find yourself in the company of Venetians, rather than fellow tourists, in the *bacari*, convivial wine bars used for a quick refreshment and snack. They are most numerous in San Polo (one of the six *sestieri*, or districts, which make up Venice), which means a stroll from San Marco *sestiere* over the Rialto bridge and through the wonderful, vibrant food market (the products of which will be turned into some of the best meals in Venice – not usually,

as we shall see, for consumption by the likes of you and me, but a treat reserved for insiders).

For anyone at all interested in food and drink, this is the area to hang out and relax. Try Vini da Pinto (Campo della Pescheria 367), a *bacaro* frequented by those who work at the fish market, or the more famous Ai Do Mori (San Polo 429), festooned with copper pots and pans. Or just try the first one you come across, check out the welcome (which will be among the warmest in the city), order an *ombra*, a small glass of wine, or a Port, perfectly acceptable as an aperitif in these parts, and some *cichetti*, the small snacks that are the Venetian version of tapas. You may be offered sautéed pota-toes, fried shrimp, fish pastes on toast, *crostini*, hams, tiny *tramezzini* (sandwiches) of crab or aubergine - you may even find it will be among the best food you will eat in the city.

Of course, many doubt that quality food of any kind is available in Venice. This is not the case. There is awful food in the city, particularly at those restaurants that fly more flags on the menu than the UN building. Establishments such as Da Fiore, Alla Madonna, La Furatola and Da Ivo are on hand to restore the city's tarnished reputation, but it is true that places of such quality are remarkably thin on the water for an Italian city.

Part of the problem is that the Venetians are not great nighthawks, so regular dining out is not on the locals' agenda. In fact, you will find this is a city that sleeps almost as soon as the sun goes down (perhaps a hangover from the days when a wrong turn in the dark after a few drinks meant at best a thorough soaking). The great food of Venice is cooked at home for the family or at elaborate dinner parties. You see, not all those *palazzi* that line the canals have become the headquarters of banks or television stations, and on the street and in the bars you will hear rumours of extravagant banquets held in sumptuous private apartments, under great chandeliers hanging from impossibly high ceilings, witnessed by the

In the most humble surroundings the average Venetian mamma can turn the booty from the food and fish markets into the finest pastas, risottos, fried fish and soups.

Above: the lagoon as seen from the gardens of the Hotel Cipriani
Right: rooms with a view at the Gothic Vendramin Palace

family's great works of art, cossetted from the *hoi polloi* searching the *calli* for the comparatively meagre pickings of the public restaurants. Here, the favoured few might dine on *granseola* (crabmeat with oil, lemon and parsley), *risi in cavroman* (rice with a cinnamon-flavoured lamb sauce) and *torresani allo spiedo* (bacon-wrapped pigeons flavoured with rosemary, juniper berries and bay leaves, served with polenta).

But it isn't only the *beau monde* who eat well. In more humble surroundings the average Venetian mamma can turn the booty from the *Erberia* and *Pescheria* (fruit and vegetable and fish markets) into the finest risottos, pastas, fried fish, and mussel soups. On your trips across the lagoon you will see the forlorn wooden frames from which dangle what must be thousands of miles of rope, all supporting the clusters of mussels whose final resting place will be in a tasty *zuppa con cozze* (mussel soup).

But short of stopping strangers on the street and begging to be taken home to mamma to try her *bisato alla Veneziana* (sautéed eel), the rest of us have to make do, which is, if the credit card is robust enough, no great hardship.

If you are still propping up Harry's Bar, a move into the restaurant will reward you with highest quality *pasta e fagioli* (pasta and bean) soup, Venetian liver, cuttlefish with polenta, or the underwhelmingly named, but delicious *risi e bisi* - rice with peas. Opposite the entrance to Harry's Bar is the Monaco and Grand Canal hotel, where you can dine on the terrace, overlooking the canal, off the finest china and linen, and where, consequently, good food would be an unexpected bonus. Well, it is more than a pleasant surprise - the crab ravioli was almost worth the plane fare to Venice alone.

If you are tired of San Marco, don't give up on Harry and the Cipriani clan just yet. Catch a *vaporetto* number 5 over to Fondamenta Sant' Eufemia, south across the canal on Giudecca. Here is Harry's Dolce, a kind of diffusion restaurant, Emporio Harry perhaps, where the same dishes as across the water cost almost half as much, and where the chocolate *torta* and the *gelati* are just as fine, and you can dine on the canal with views across to the Dorsoduro *sestiere*.

Still on Giudecca, but along on the eastern tip, is the Hotel Cipriani, perhaps the most special of a whole raft of special hotels in Venice (although loud and justified protests will doubtless rise from the peeved portals of the Danieli, the Gritti Palace and the Monaco at such a wild accusation). But the Cipriani scores by being set apart from the hordes of San Marco, serenely waiting for its children to be shuttled across to its three-acre oasis.

Whether it is lunch in the garden, a Bellini in the bar (yes, I would have one here), or dinner in the Fortuny-patterned dining room, the Hotel Cipriani prides itself on immaculate service for those who have made the four-minute crossing. Check out the wine list, lovingly put together by Victor Hazan. If that name is familiar, it is because Victor is the husband of Marcella Hazan, the grand diva of Italian *cucina* who, as well as being the author of a quartet of definitive Italian cookbooks (the inspiration, and the basis, for the menus of hundreds of modish restaurants across the world), also ran a highly regarded cookery school, where you could learn all those skills that the city likes to keep behind closed doors.

Tagliata di filetto di manzo con purè di spinaci al peperoncino

800g cooked spinach
400g single cream
100g Parmesan cheese
1800g fillet of beef
100g butter
50g extra virgin olive oil
2 pieces of hot red chilli
400g Sandeman Founder's Reserve Port
400g veal stock
salt and pepper

Serves 10

Mince the spinach and squeeze out excess moisture.
Reduce the cream by half by fast boiling and add the spinach
and the chilli. Stir well and cook to a thick purée.
Stir in the Parmesan cheese and season to taste. Keep warm.
Season the meat with salt and pepper. Heat the oil
and 50g of the butter and quickly seal the meat on both sides,
then cook for 5-8 minutes (according to taste) turning once.
Remove from the pan and keep warm. Deglaze the pan with
Port and reduce to a quarter by fast boiling.
Stir in veal stock, then reduce gently to required consistency.
Season to taste, and stir in remaining butter.

Spoon a little spinach purée on to the centre of each plate.
Cut the beef into slices and arrange around the spinach.
Spoon the sauce over and serve at once.

Recommended wine: Barolo, Brunello di Montalcino or Sassicaia

Sautéed Fillet of Beef served with a Spicy Spinach Purée
Renato Piccolotto. Head Chef, Hotel Cipriani

The presence of Port on the list, however, probably owes much to Dr Rusconi, the Hotel Cipriani's Managing Director, who fell in love with the wine in London. 'There are pubs near The Savoy, where I worked during the Seventies, that specialise in Port. At The Savoy they didn't feed me, so in the morning, evening or afternoon – depending on the shift – I would take a glass of Port in one of them instead of a meal.' Nor was he alone in this practice. 'I was joined by, shall we say, professional ladies of the area, who enjoyed a similar habit.'

These days Dr Rusconi doesn't have to skip meals, but Port still plays a role in his diet - he encourages his kitchen to use it, 'Zabaglione, for instance, is far better cooked with Port.' His wife, Connie, thinks this is a waste. 'Absolutely not,' says the doctor, 'You should use only the best liquor for cooking.'

Even if you are not staying at the Hotel Cipriani (and that credit card has to be fighting fit for this one), it doesn't matter how late you linger over the Port, be it in a dish of *zabaglione* or in your glass, the launches run 24 hours. Don't leave it too late, remember the Accademia closes at 2pm, so an early start the next day will be essential. But then, when a host like Dr Rusconi pushes you to another Port, it is hard to say no. Perhaps the Tintorettos can wait after all.

Zabaglione al porto stravecchio

8 egg yolks
150ml Sandeman 20-Year-Old Tawny Port
100g caster sugar
4 bitter Saronno macaroons

Serves 4

Put the egg yolks, the Port and the sugar in a cone-shaped copper container.
With a whisk whip the mixture until you get a light foam. Then cook in a *bain-marie*, while still whisking, until you obtain a thick and smooth cream. Place in 4 crystal glasses, then crumble a macaroon on top of each glass.

Serve at once, very hot, with a glass of chilled Sandeman 20-Year-Old Tawny Port

Zabaglione with 20-Year-Old Tawny Port
Renato Piccolotto. Head Chef, Hotel Cipriani

'...when a host like Dr Rusconi pushes you to another port, it is hard to say no. Perhaps the Tintorettos can wait after all.'

Orient Express

Don't let anyone fob you off with some cockamamie idea that the Orient Express has anything to do with travel. That's an absurd notion. If all you want to do is to leave Venice and get back to work, there are ways and means of doing it that take half the time, for a fraction of the cost.

No, the real reason for running a comb through your hair and packing your best clothes is food. Yes, of course the scenery is to die for: an epic, cinematic parade of mountains, valleys and forests, baroque cities, and pastures. But after a few hours you can get blasé about another snow-capped peak or medieval church spire. That's when your nervous system latches on to the aroma of freshly ground coffee coming from the galley and the only sound you want to hear is the Chief Steward call dinner.

This over-dressed art deco train with a style of inlaid marquetry and Lalique glass, polished brass, fringed lamp shades and starched white linen, that might have slipped through an H.G.Wells' time vortex, is just one great big restaurant-on-wheels. Mile after mile and meal after meal; a lock-in for a day and a half with nothing to do but imagine the next course and sleep off the one before. You can't go anywhere or do anything on board a shrine to food except, of course, eat.

Nobody admits to such zealous over-indulgence. On a train renowned for a different sort of taste the passengers say one thing and mean another. 'I come to forget,' says Geraldine. Her hair in a French pleat, fragrant and self-contained in the way that English women from the Home Counties are. She takes herself on a round trip to Venice every June. She sits at the same table, the one furthest from the galley, facing the back of the train, and orders her Port in time for the crossing of the Italian/Austrian frontier.

'I think I read about someone who did this. I can't remember where,' she says. Any other thoughts are confined to a leather-bound notebook always at her side.

There are staff to attend to your every need

Most passengers climb aboard for the exact opposite; they travel on the Orient Express to remember things: weddings; anniversaries and birthdays. I even heard of a couple who wrote to the company to express their profound thanks that after years of endeavouring to start a family, their first child was born nine months after their trip. It might have been the romance of travel of course, although I'm inclined to think it was the food.

A lunch of John Dory, garnished with a compote of apple and ginger, is served as we leave Verona, the first stop after Venice. There is an afternoon tea of Viennese pastries, scones and jam with strawberries the size of walnuts as we slip into the Austrian Alps, caviar, *foie gras* and medallions of veal with a lobster sauce as the magenta cloak of sunset envelopes Lake Constance.

I swapped my strawberry cream dessert chocolate for one with a marzipan centre whilst inside my head I orchestrated the rhythm of the tracks. A scruffy dog tending sheep barks at the train and women picking flowers look up. Then I must have fallen asleep. Real pleasure can have that effect.

Chef Christian Bodiguel has telephone cards for every country we pass through and a comprehensive list of all his suppliers. If you pass the galley you can hear him jabbering away over the din of the tracks as we rattle across Europe. At each station there is something new waiting for his inspection: fresh bread at Zurich, and lobsters, langoustines and crates of

fish in Paris. M.Bodiguel prods and pokes it all before agreeing to take it on board.

'I think it's my sense of adventure,' he says. 'I love to cook and I love to travel and every journey is different' - so much so that he cannot guarantee what will be on each day's menu until he's stepped down on to the platform and given it the once-over. His one insistence is that all his ingredients are completely fresh. After one particularly galling three-hour delay M.Bodiguel has designed a *menu de secours*. It made me hope for a signal failure so that I could sample his emergency supplies: *confit de canard*, haricots and tins of pears, and bottles of Ruby Port for *Poire Hélène*.

'I say it's a challenge,' he says. 'So many nationalities, so many tastes.' An added bonus is the fact that his clients cannot get up and go somewhere else. But it's a testament to his skill and diplomatically correct cuisine that the Orient Express is such a culinary success.

There is a sense of occasion on this train that even the jabber and camera flash of flocks of Japanese tourists, desperate to capture every minute detail on celluloid, cannot diminish. The cut glasses tinkle gently in the bar and little children wave from the distance as the waiter produces another plate. It's brunch this time: scrambled eggs and smoked salmon with something chilled and flinty from Burgundy.

He bows, I nod. The waiter refills Geraldine's glass and the others diners smile at each other; another meal and another mile slip by effortlessly.

'The scenery is parade of baroque cities

to die for: an epic, cinematic mountains, valleys and forests, and pastures.'

Côte d'Azur
Cannes
Cap
d'Antibes
Cap Ferrat
Nice
Portofino
Villefranche
Antibes

Henri Matisse *Grand Masque* 1948. Aquatinte 43.3 x 34.8 cm Musée Matisse,Nice © Succession H Matisse/DACS 1996

The view from La Croisette in Cannes pans out like a Dufy painting: a perfect blue-green sea, a large, white sailing ship against the unblemished horizon, and a distant, tree-covered island, beyond a promenade lined with wicker chairs. Here, white-haired ladies, who retreat south each year from Paris, sit and watch the world go by. Bronzed bodies lie under striped umbrellas on the hotels' private beaches, and along the pavement, immaculately groomed poodles strut in time with their Versace-clad owners.

Few places merge the old and the new with such ease as the Riviera. Despite the inevitable sprouting of high-rise buildings, the Côte d'Azur has retained its elegance and style. 'Who knows? Maybe they are beautiful too,' said Picasso of the new developments when he returned here in old age. Surprisingly, the modern world, including roller-blading youths, doesn't look out of place against the turn-of-the-century backdrop, from the flaking pink villas of Portofino in Italy, to the elegant, wedding-cake façade of the Carlton Hotel in Cannes, where Cary Grant and Grace Kelly would be as at home as ever.

Bernard Rousseau has worked as a concierge at the Carlton Hotel for 34 years. 'People still think of this as a place where only kings and maharajas stay, which is how it used to be,' he says wistfully. 'They would come in their tuxedos with 30 pieces of luggage each. Now it's blue jeans and trainers. But it is still a magical place, and the view has remained unchanged.'

It was in the old town that Lord Brougham, a former British chancellor, arrived in 1834, and founded Cannes as a resort for the rich. He loved the climate, and the British aristocracy quickly caught on, fleeing the British fog each year for the sunny, southern winters. Its glamorous status was assured when the annual film festival was established here nearly half a century ago, and every summer since then the great names of the silver screen have swept in, pursued by *paparazzi*.

The Martinez Hotel is a glorious art deco palace in the middle of La Croisette. James McKissic, the cocktail bar pianist, has played here for generations of stars from Brigitte Bardot to Bruce Willis. 'When I saw Liza Minnelli in here, I started playing *Cabaret* out of respect,' says McKissic, as he strums out a few bars from the musical on his grand piano. 'She looked over and smiled, and that was all I needed. She knew I was playing for her.'

Up the stairway is the Palme d'Or restaurant, where summer visitors brave the *paparazzi* to sample some of the finest food on the Riviera. Christian Willer, the Head Chef, is adept at using Port in his recipes, particularly to give warmth and flavour to winter dishes. 'It can enhance sweetness, especially in sauces, and with fruit. Just a little Port can transform the dish.'

Before the British arrived to winter on the Côte d'Azur, it was little more than a series of fortress towns and fishing communities. Artists still paint beneath the 16th century clock tower in Cannes, where wedding couples pose for portraits under the eucalyptus trees. Across the water lies L'Ile Sainte Marguerite, where you can still see the ruins of the prison that once held The Man in the Iron Mask, the legendary French prisoner whose murals remain on the walls of his former cell. His true identity is an unsolved mystery, but more than 60 names have been suggested, including Molière, Cromwell's son and Louis XIV's brother.

It was not until the 1920s that the Riviera was transformed into a summer resort for the rich and fashionable. After the wealthy British and Russian visitors had turned it into a second home, the Americans arrived, and it was they who decided to stay long after winter had passed. It was here, in 1923, that the sun-tan first became chic, when Coco Chanel emerged on the gangway of the Duke of Westminster's yacht, with her skin bronzed to a rich, golden brown.

Another visitor, Prince Jean-Louis de Faucigny-Lucinge, who took his bride to the Riviera as part of their honeymoon, later recalled the event when his eyes fell on the sun-tanned Ms Chanel. 'I think she may have invented sunbathing, at that time she invented everything,' he said. 'It was delicious…We immediately started sunbathing…It was a study, it took time, hours and hours of sunbathing.'

Previous page: view from La Croisette, Cannes. Left and above: the L'Ile Sainte Marguerite, across the water from Cannes, where you can still see the ruins of the prison that once held The Man in the Iron Mask

Clockwise from above: The Carlton Hotel; hitting the road - Riviera-style;
view from a Carlton Hotel bedroom; the public beach at Cannes

'People still think of this as a place where only kings and maharajas stay, which is how it used to be. They would come in their tuxedos with 30 pieces of luggage each.'

Le soufflé de prunes Reine Claude au porto

12 greengage plums
120g caster sugar
1 glass of Sandeman Tawny Port
30g softened butter
30g sifted flour
8 eggs
Serves 4

Simmer the greengage plums in Port. Add caster sugar while they are cooking. When the plums are tender, remove from the pan and reduce the remaining liquid until the juice thickens. Melt the butter with the flour and add all of the remaining juice from the cooked plums, and place over the heat.
Bring to boil. When cool, add the egg yolks and fold in the whisked egg whites. Pour the mixture into the soufflé moulds until they are half full, layer with the cooked plums and then fill the dishes with the remaining mixture. Cook in the oven at a medium high temperature for 20-25 minutes, until the soufflé is golden and has risen.

Dust with icing sugar. Serve with the remaining Port sauce at the table, pierce a hole in the centre and pour in the warm sauce immediately.

Recommended wine: 20-Year-Old Tawny Port or Black Muscat

Plum Soufflé with Port
Christian Willer. Head Chef, Hotel Martinez

Left, from the top:
the private beach and
pool at the
Hotel Martinez;
the art deco façade
of the Miramar
Opposite: views from
the old fortress at
L'Ile Sainte Marguerite

F Scott Fitzgerald captured the spell of the Côte d'Azur in the 1930s. His vision in *Tender is the Night* was based on the 'happy few' who turned the region, with its old-style palace hotels, into the world's most exclusive summer resort.

'On the pleasant shore of the French Riviera, about half-way between Marseilles and the Italian border, stands a large, proud, rose-coloured hotel,' he wrote in the opening of the novel. 'Deferential palms cool its flushed façade, and before it stretches a short, dazzling beach.'

Fitzgerald was describing the Hotel du Cap Eden Roc, in Antibes Juan les Pins, where he would sit in the restaurant, Champagne glass in hand, and watch Zelda, his doomed and beautiful wife, diving into the sea. Today the hotel remains a Mecca for the glamorous and wealthy. Set in 22 acres of elegant gardens, with 300 metres of its own coastline, the hotel attracts the most glittering stars during the Cannes Film Festival. Among the recent 'happy few' to stay here are Nicole Kidman, who took daily walks in the rose-filled gardens; Johnny Depp, who found it hard to choose between a suite in the main building and rooms on the edge of the sea; and Hugh Grant and Elizabeth Hurley, who opted for a suite overlooking the water. Guests have to pass an unofficial exclusivity test to reside at Eden Roc. At the height of the season demand always outweighs supply, and the hotel, which only accepts payment in cash, can effectively choose who stays here, which allows it to opt for the most glamorous guests. The manager, Jean-Claude Irondelle, known as the 'King of Eden Roc', recently delighted in informing the head of American Express that he did not accept credit cards. 'We don't have to,' he says, smiling. Equally exclusive is Le Grand Hotel du Cap Ferrat, further along the coast, where room rates start at around £400 a night. 'People who have a lot of money want to be with their own kind, that is where they are comfortable,' says John Rebmann, the manager, commenting candidly on how the Riviera has retained so much of its

allure for the wealthy. The food at Le Grand is appropriately splendid, served either on the elegant terrace, or beside the spectacular swimming pool, which can be reached by cable car, and which appears to be overflowing into the sea. One of the Riviera's best-known figures, Pierre Gruneberg, has been teaching swimming at Le Grand for 45 years. He has given lessons to many of the great and the good who have passed through the South of France, and they have all signed his *livre d'or*. There are doodles by Picasso, Cocteau and César, as well as messages from more recent stars. '*Merci pour tous les sorties de la mer. C'est magnifique*,' wrote Robin Williams. 'Me and the missus thank you for some laughs,' wrote Paul McCartney. Gruneberg's favourite pupil was Charlie Chaplin's daughter, Victoria. 'We fell in love,' he says. 'I was 28 years old, she was only five. Once she wrote me a letter which said: "You will never love me as much as I love you." Years later when she had grown up and married a circus manager, I met her again at one of their shows, but she didn't remember me.'

Near the hotel is one of the greatest monuments to the 'old money' of the Riviera. The Villa Ephrussi de Rothschild was built by Madame Ephrussi, a member of the French branch of the famous banking family, who lived there for only a few years before moving and loaning the house out to her friends. The extraordinary pink mansion overlooks sweeping gardens of classical lawns and lily ponds stretching towards the sea in the shape of a ship's deck. Her gardeners used to have to wear sailor uniforms to tend the vast expanse of flowers. This is also where Cary Grant chased the diamond robber in *To Catch a Thief*.

Other stars prefer the more discreet luxury of the private villas. Sheikhs and princes have built their own summer palaces in the mountains in the area, behind the main town, known as Super-Cannes. The coastline around Cap d'Antibes is dotted with grand houses such as the dusty pink Villa Nelleric, where the filmmakers Ismail Merchant and James Ivory play host to their actors during the Film Festival.

Porto & foie gras

2 escalopes (100g) of *foie gras* cru
2 figs
20g butter
Sauce:
100g white onions, finely chopped
100g butter
32cl Sandeman Ruby Port
32cl veal stock
salt and pepper

laurel leaves

Serves 2-4

Season escalopes with salt and pepper, and cook quickly in a very hot oven, for 5 to 10 minutes. Place them on absorbent paper. Cut each fig into the shape of a cross, and heat under the grill for 10 minutes before serving.

For the sauce: Brown the finely chopped onions in butter and add the Port. Partly reduce it, and add the veal stock. Reduce again by half, and bring to the boil again with the remaining butter. Season to taste.

To serve: Put the separate pieces of fig back together again, on top of the escalopes, and pour over the Port sauce with the onions. Decorate with fresh laurel leaves.

Escalopes de Foie Gras de Canard aux Figues Sauce Porto.
Escalopes of *foie gras* of duck with figs in Port sauce.
Recommended wine: chilled Sandeman 20-Year-Old Tawny Port

Jean-Claude Guillon, Chef de Cuisine, Grand Hotel du Cap-Ferrat

Homard aux choux verts sauce porto

400/500g lobster
100ml olive oil
150g green cabbage
50g carrots
50g celery
1 chopped tomato
50g courgettes

For the sauce
50g white onions, finely chopped
75g butter
16cl Sandeman Ruby Port
16cl veal stock

Serves 1

Boil salted water and plunge the lobster into the pan for 10 minutes. Remove and shell it, once cool, keeping the pieces of the shell for decoration. Brown the lobster in olive oil and leave it to simmer gently for another 10 minutes. Slice the green cabbage and blanche in salted water until it is lightly crunchy. Cook the carrots, celery, tomato and courgettes lightly in salted water.

For the sauce: Brown the finely chopped onions in 50g of butter, add the Port, partly reduce it and add the veal stock. Reduce again by half and bring it to boil with the remaining butter. Season to taste.

To serve: Melt remaining 25g of butter, add the cabbage and vegetables and toss. In the middle of a plate make a circle with the vegetables, put the lobster tail and the claws on both sides. Decorate with the head and surround with the Port sauce.

Recommended wine: a full-bodied Chardonnay such as Puligny Montrachet

Lobster with Green Cabbage in a Port sauce.
Jean-Claude Guillon,
Chef de Cuisine, Grand Hotel du Cap-Ferrat

The faded elegant lounge opens on to gardens that lead down to a swimming pool and an outside bar, and a private jetty where dinner guests arrive by boat. Only a small corner of the Riviera has been completely overwhelmed by the modern world; the fierce growl of traffic along the Promenade des Anglais in Nice is more reminiscent of the M1 motorway than the *Belle Epoque*. But the flower market in the old town is charming, and the Negresco, one of the last, great, privately owned hotels in the world, is an unmissable temple of kitsch. Elton John has stayed here, and The Beatles wrote the lyrics to *The Fool on the Hill* in the main suite.

Each level has a different historical theme, such as the reign of Napoleon I on the fourth floor, where the Imperial Suite is decorated in rich red silks, a leopard-skin carpet and a portrait of the great French leader. The bathrooms have suites varnished with glitter, in different shades from apricot to blue, and there is a carousel restaurant where horses rotate above the tables to fairground music. 'It's the Negresco. You love it or you hate it, but you can't be indifferent,' says Dominque Le Stanc, the hotel's head chef and its one indisputable treasure. The food is superb: open ravioli with artichokes, asparagus and langoustines, chocolate pudding made of clouds of the lightest sponge in almond cream, or his celebrated sorbet presented as a musical stave. The Negresco also has a fine collection of Port. 'In France it is drunk at room temperature with cheese at the end of a meal,' says Patrick Millereau, chief sommelier. 'Or we take it chilled as an aperitif. We tend to prefer White Port. Often I encourage people to try a good Port instead of a dessert wine. They are very surprised when they taste how good it is.' His cellar includes a 1900 Vintage. 'It is a great pleasure to open that bottle. You have a lot of sediment, and you have to open it very slowly because the cork is like powder.'

Perhaps the most startling contrast to the brash glory of the Negresco is the Hotel Splendido in Portofino, which is reached by a dramatic drive through the mountain tunnels of Monaco and across the border into Italy.

Gruneberg's favourite pupil was Charlie Chaplin's daughter, Victoria. 'We fell in love,' he says. 'I was 28 years old, she was five. She wrote me a letter which said: "You will never love me as much as I love you." '

Left: the dramatic coastline of Cap d'Antibes. Above: the gardens of Villa Ephrussi de Rothschild

Truffes au porto

For the poultry stock:
500g poultry carcass
2.5cl peanut oil
100g chopped shallots
5g garlic
1 bouquet garni
40cl Sandeman Ruby Port
12cl red wine
4 x 30g truffles
750ml brown veal stock
salt and ground black pepper
one egg yolk
250g flour

Serves 4

Brown the poultry carcasses in the oven with the peanut oil.
Add the chopped shallots, garlic and bouquet garni.
Cook gently until they are browned at a medium high
temperature. Deglaze with a little of the Port and the red
wine. Remove the poultry carcasses, and reduce to a sauce.
Add the veal stock and reduce again by half, then put
through a sieve.

Prepare 4 small oval terracotta casseroles with lids
(10cm x 7cm x 5cm). In each casserole, place one truffle
of 30g, 1 soup spoon of Port, 3 soup spoons of the
chicken stock and some black pepper.
Cover with the lids. Mix 250g of flour with 100ml of cold
water to make a wet paste. Divide into four rolls, and place
them around the edge of each casserole, to seal the lid
and the dish. Glaze with egg yolk. It will harden and prevent
the steam from escaping during cooking.
Place the sealed casseroles in the oven and bake for
40 minutes at a medium to high temperature.
Take the casseroles directly to the table, break the golden
crust, lift the cover and slowly inhale!

Recommended wine: Vintage Port

Truffles with Port

Roger Vergé, Head Chef/Proprietor, Le Moulin de Mougins

Main picture and bottom right: The Carousel Room
at Hotel Negresco Top right and centre: the Napoleon Suite

Above and opposite: the terracotta houses of Portofino

The Splendido, a converted monastery, stands on a cliff overlooking the sea and the rustic fishing village of Portofino. The wrought-iron balconies are partly obscured by 150-year-old wisteria, which forms a colourful roof over the terrace restaurant. Purple bougainvillaea hangs over the walls, and the air is heavy with the scent of jasmine.

In the leather-bound visitors' book you can see the names of Edward and Wallis Simpson, Rex Harrison, Clarke Gable, Humphrey Bogart, Lauren Bacall, Elizabeth Taylor and Richard Burton... You can still sit on the terrace, as they may have done, to drink a Bellini. The guests may be different, but the view has remained unchanged: the Splendido overlooks Castillo Brown where *Enchanted April* was filmed, and in between are dark green woodlands, a cluster of pink villas and a church tower. Below is the tiny port that looks like an opera set, with terracotta and ochre houses decorated in *trompe l'oeil*, and fishing boats almost hidden between the luxury cruisers. In recent years the Splendido has welcomed an array of stars including Annie Lennox, U2, and Madonna who wrote to the staff: 'Get my room ready, I'm coming back.' When Rod Stewart visited from his private yacht, Antonio Becalli, the barman, served him Port on the terrace as an aperitif. Stewart then delighted guests by singing for them. Becalli is well aware of Port's reputation for loosening vocal chords, and has since invented his own White Port cocktail, made with Bacardi, Cointreau, egg white and White Port, served chilled with a cherry. After a drink in the dusky evening light, dinner is served on the terrace overlooking the garden.

The other great legacy of the Riviera was left by the artists who flocked here, before it was taken over by film stars. You can still find many of the works of painters and sculptors from Matisse to Miro. ' When I realised that every morning I would see this light again, I couldn't believe my luck,' said Matisse of his arrival in Nice in 1917. His paintings hang at the Matisse Museum in Cimiez, the smart residential area of Nice, where they appear alongside the objects that inspired them, such as the famous red-striped chair. A little way up the mountains, in Vence, is the Dominican chapel he painted, to thank the nuns who cared for him when he was sick. The simple black outline of a Dominican priest is dramatic against the pristine white walls and bright blue, green and yellow windows. 'I want those who come into my chapel to be purified,' Matisse said. But Picasso commented sceptically that it looked like a bathroom.

In Villefranche-sur-Mer, another church bears the signature of a great artist. The 14th century St Peter's chapel was decorated by Cocteau between 1956 and 1957. His distinctive figures, lightly shaded, are powerful in the modest setting. Behind the stone altar is the image of Peter walking on water, unaware that two angels are holding him up.

Cocteau was a regular at Mère Germaine's, one of the best fish restaurants on the Riviera, and a favourite haunt of American soldiers after the Second World War. Josiane Blouin, the daughter of the original *mère*, still has her mother's letters from the artist. On July 29, 1957, he wrote: 'The Monsignor of Nice is going to bless the chapel. Put on your best hat and come.'

Further up the mountains, in St Paul de Vence, is the Colombe d'Or, the rustic old stone inn where many great artists, including Picasso, Braque and Matisse, would come and exchange paintings for meals. The dining room is full of their works, and the terrace is decorated with sculptures and mosaics. Towards the end of his life, when he was almost infirm, Matisse would still visit the hotel, and a waiter would come out to serve him coffee through his car window.

2 tsps of Dijon mustard
1 sprig of local herbs
1 sprig of rosemary
3 glasses of Sandeman White Port
20 small pieces of lamb
200g rocket leaves
salt and pepper
3 laurel leaves

Serves 4

Costolette d'agnello marinate al porto

In a small metal pan mix the mustard and herbs with the Port to make a marinade. Place the lamb pieces in the marinade, and leave them to soak for 2 hours.

Place the lamb pieces in a separate oval oven-proof dish and grill for 3 minutes. Bring the marinade to the boil separately. Place the lamb on a bed of rocket leaves on a round serving dish. Pour the marinade on top, garnish with laurel leaves and serve hot.

Recommended wine: claret, Château Labegorce Zede

Lamb marinated in Port
Snr Pizzi, Head Chef, Hotel Splendido

Madonna wrote to the staff at the Hotel Splendido: 'Get my room ready, I'm coming back.'

Wonderful hotel
wonderful people
I deeply regret leaving
Sincerely
Groucho Marx

Left: Paintings by Picasso, Matisse
and Braque (pictured) would be exchanged
for meals at the Colombe D'Or
(Georges Braque ©ADAGP,
Paris and DACS, London 1996)
Above: Jean Cocteau decorated the
Chapelle Saint Pierre
(left) in Villefranche-Sur-Mer (right)

'He regarded
the sculptures
as his friends.
He didn't
much like
having his
paintings
around
unless he was
working on
them, but the
sculptures
surrounded
him. He
liked their
company.'

John Golding, Artist

The Musée Picasso at Antibes. Left: Pablo Picasso, *Woman's Head with Chignon* Boisgeloup 1931-32 © Succession Picasso / DACS 1996

The grave of Marc Chagall lies in a nearby chapel, beneath an apricot tree, overlooking the tiny villages that pan out towards the distant sea.

But the most striking gallery on the Côte d'Azur is the Picasso Museum in Antibes, set in the 16th century Grimaldi Castle, where the artist had a studio from 1946 until his death in 1973. Beside it is the church where Picasso, aged 65 and about to be a father again, told his lover, Françoise Gilot: 'Swear that you'll love me forever.' Inside are some of his greatest works, including *Joie de Vivre*. Nearby is the Golfe-Juan beach where followers from across the world sought him out. Raymond Mason, the artist who met Picasso there in the 1950s, witnessed his sunbathing trips. 'I arrived just before Picasso and saw the transformation of this normal beach into his court, with all these people coming up to talk to him.'

The only way to conclude a visit to the castle is to return back to the other great French art, food. Le Moulin de Mougins, in Mougins, where Picasso finally retired to rid himself of his fans, remains one of the most famous restaurants in the south of France. The chef, Roger Vergé, prepares truffles in Port in the delightful setting of the converted mill.

One of the finest treats of the Riviera, however, comes at La Terrasse, the Juana Hotel's restaurant in Antibes, where Christian Morisset, the head chef, who is as famous for his handlebar moustache as for his cooking, is preparing fish, gathering his ingredients before him like an artist creating a still life. Afterwards, François Barrache, the owner of the hotel and a celebrated Port lover, indulges his passion for the drink in the afternoon sun.

'A man's tastes change in life,' he says. 'My taste in wine and in food is different from when I was young. But Port, I know, is a constant pleasure that I shall enjoy always, just like this.'

John Dory au porto rouge

4 fillets of John Dory fish
a little olive oil
4 small white onions
40cl Sandeman Ruby Port
a splash of balsamic vinegar
salt and ground black pepper
8 cherry tomatoes
a knob of butter

Serves 2

Cover the fillets on one side with black pepper (leaving the skin on the other) then fry the fish lightly in olive oil.
In a separate pan, cook the chopped onions in olive oil with the Port.
Reduce this with a splash of balsamic vinegar and a knob of butter.
Place the onions in the middle of a plate, and arrange the fillets in a star shape.
Skin the tomatoes, trickle a little olive oil over them, and place around the fish. Pour the Port sauce around the side of the plate and serve.

John Dory in Ruby Port

Recommended wine: Rosé Reuilly

Christian Morisset (pictured left), Head chef, La Terrasse

Antwerp

I could walk around Antwerp forever. It's one of those *easy* cities - on the eyes and on the feet. No hills, no size at all really, just shadowy courtyards and bars where the waitresses don't care if you order a drink or stare out of a window all day.

It's not one of those places that you crash into with a bang and depart drained and exhausted, your skin like parchment and your liver begging for a quick and painless death. It's much too civilised, too old, too refined, too dignified and nowadays much, much too cool. It doesn't have New York's mesmerising skyline, or the seductive beauty of Paris, or the pomp and circumstance of London. Don't expect involuntary intakes of breath as you step out of the baroque Central Station. For one thing, it's much smaller than those other places. The capital of Flanders is David to Brussels' Goliath, its 400,000 or so inhabitants living in an area that is walkable in a single morning, and its buildings, with a few notable exceptions, on a more human scale, both physically and aesthetically.

It has its fair share of beauties. The Wagnerian Koninklijk Museum (of Fine Arts) with its golden chariots; the old and leathery Plantin-Moretus Museum and, of course, the cathedral. It's rare when you can't make out its heavily embellished spire, like some grey, Gothic rocket ship, prodding the marble sky. Better than any street sign, it guides you home, whatever condition you're in.

Then there are the Renaissance craftsmens' houses, with tiny gold statues on the pinnacles of stepped roofs, ornate pediments, carved architraves and leaded lights, facing on to Grote Markt in the heart of the city centre. And there are dozens of dimly lit cul-de-sacs and secret gardens. Venture south and you'll find Corbusier-influenced modernist blocks, and across the tram tracks, just beyond the south eastern border of the '19th century belt', is Cogles Osy Lei, an estate of renovated art nouveau homes as fancy as any wedding cake.

In a city where the car has been tamed, people stroll or cycle. It's quieter still on Saturdays when people sleep late after a long, late Friday night out.

To get to grips with Antwerp, get under its skin and find out what makes it tick, the first thing you should do is ditch the guide book (you can read that on the plane home) and get walking. Step off the well-trodden tourist path, with its restaurants selling buckets of mussels, and fries smothered in mayonnaise, and head... well south is as good a place to start as any. This is where you're going to find the new Antwerp, the city that has defied all the odds and emerged as the street-fashion capital of Europe.

The 'south' is only a brisk 20-minute stroll from the city centre. Along Kloosterstraat, the umbilical chord between the old and the new(er), well-dressed shops offering designer clothes and Belgian chocolates give way to cavernous emporiums of 20th century style. This is the markets of Camden, Portobello and Clignancourt, and the Lower East Side all rolled into one. Further on, the scrubland between Waalse Kaai and Vlaamse Kaai were docks until the mid-Sixties, when they were filled in to provide an open space for the Whitsun Fair which is held each May and June for six weeks.

Three decades on this is the nerve centre of south Antwerp. There are galleries that look like the sort of modish homes featured in Sunday supplements and kitchen shops that resemble galleries. Restaurants that are a match for anything in London's Notting Hill or New York's Greenwich Village are packed until the early hours, and in the summer months tables and chairs spill out into the streets. The music drifts seamlessly from hip hop to reggae, and even the dogs sport pony-tails.

What I like are the shadowy bars and restaurants where people hang out talking until the early hours. Places like Bar Tabac, cobbled together on a shoestring by Saskea, a 23-year-old jewellery designer who set up her earthy, 'French' bar to finance her work. The bar itself is an upturned cupboard and a bed knocked together, the floor resembles an excavation and on the terrace no two chairs are alike. But it's as funky as hell and crammed after midnight.

Saskea, dark and smiling and about as pretentious as a half of bitter, parks her battered old Datsun out front.

'I wanted it to be in the south because it's not so touristy,' she says. 'Here the people are more interesting. But the most important thing is the intimacy between the people and the bar.'

If Bar Tabac gets too hot, as it can do on Fridays when the fashion crowd breezes in, I may stroll over the *kaai* to Entrepôt du Congo for a late bowl of fresh pasta, and watch the comings and goings in the mirrors on every wall.

Then I might take a walk down to the waterfront and sip Port taken from a barrel at De Negen Vaten. It takes a while for your eyes to adjust to the darkness in this hole-in-the-wall that only closes 'when the last customer has emptied his glass,' says owner Orhan Esen. As he slices spicy *chorizo* sausages, he says he thought he was running a Spanish bar, but has to acknowledge the irony in the fact that his most popular drinks, after *sangria*, are the Tawny and Ruby Ports on tap.

You find Port all over the city. Sandeman is in evidence at De Witte Lelie (The White Lily), a cool, white residence in the centre of town, run with impeccable style by manageress Caroline Bocq, and also in the post-modernist Dock's Café overlooking the river. Port of every description is offered prominently as an accompaniment to Belgian cheese, strangely complementing the long velvet drapes and the plump, ruby-red upholstery. Chef Marc Van Tongel uses Port in his definitive Belgian restaurant, 'T Silveren Claverblat, housed in a 16th century merchant's house within earshot of the cathedral. If you tilt forward in the street outside and peer through the pavement-level window, you can see this member of Belgium's Order of Master Chefs measuring out

Gratin du mango au porto

1 mango,
2 egg yolks
2 eggshell halves of granulated sugar
2 eggshells halves of white wine
1 eggshell half of Sandeman Tawny Port
fresh mint and a few grilled almonds

Serves 2

Slice the mango and arrange into the shape of a flower. Make a *sabayon* with the egg yolks, sugar, white wine and the tawny Port. Whisk vigorously for several minutes and then cook over a medium flame until the mixture pales and thickens - it should be frothy without the eggs coagulating. Pour over the mango and grill for a few seconds until it starts to brown. Garnish with a sprig of mint and a few chopped, grilled almonds.

Gratin of Mango with Port

Recommended wine: Muscat de Revesaltes

Marc Van Tongel, Chef, 'T Silveren Claverblat

'I don't export my chocolates. Every week I get letters asking me to send them abroad. This week I got one from Kenya and another from Japan. But I say no. You cannot make chocolates of this quality in bigger numbers. If they want them, they have to come to Antwerp.'

Hans Burie

the ingredients of his *gratin du mango au Porto*, an interpretation of the classic Italian *zabaglione:* measured in eggshell halves; eggs, sugar, white wine and Tawny Port. He shows a refreshing absence of exact measurements in a dessert that relies on culinary precision.

'On its own, the Port would be too strong for the *sabayon*,' explains Van Tongel, who has lived and cooked in Antwerp for 30 years. 'But with the wine we have the same colour but a fuller flavour.'

Actually, I've just realised what I like most about the city: it's the custom, wherever you are, for serving dark chocolate with coffee: tiny, home-made slabs of chocolate and strong *espresso* coffee for a real urban shot in the arm – three or four times a day.

Belgians consume tons of chocolate; it has been estimated as much as 10 kilograms per person, per year. Chocolate-maker Hans Burie, whose family business on Gastuis Str. is a Mecca for chocoholics, confesses to 5000 kilos in 40 years himself. Eventually, his doctor told him to stop eating it and concentrate on selling the stuff instead.

Hans Burie, in his world of chocolate,
where even the wine
bottles are dark and delicious to eat

De Witte Lelie: a cool white residence...with impeccable style

'...This is a quiet place in the centre of the city. Listen, you can't hear anything. We serve Belgian chocolate and Port - you can't hurry fine Belgian chocolate or a 20-Year-Old Port; here time is of no importance.'

Caroline Bocq, manageress, De Witte Lelie

'Nobody had heard of Belgian fashion. Traditional styles, quality, yes, no problem. But *fashion* was new. Also our names were impossible to pronounce. So for us it was easier to come out as a group - then people could say 'those Belgians from Antwerp...'

Dries Van Noten

That Antwerp is on a roll is self-evident. The excitement in the media and in conversation is reminiscent of the clamour over Barcelona in the Eighties. There are more clothes shops, bars and restaurants in the south than you can shake a credit card at. In fact, so many that fashion designer Dries Van Noten, the prince of wearable style, whose fashion house 'Het Modepaleis' stands like a gatehouse to the south, has drawn up a sort of 'groove city guide' that his staff supply to the scores of foreign buyers and journalists who beat a path to his door.

His impact on Antwerp and that of other graduates from the city's fashion school - among them Dirk Bikkemberg and Ann Demeulemeester, members of the infamous Belgian Six of the mid-Eighties, cannot be overstated. Their international success during the past decade, plus the fact that they have all steadfastly refused to leave Antwerp for other 'established' fashion capitals, has given the city confidence in itself.

From his office/warehouse, piled high with boxes labelled for shops all over the world, Dries Van Noten says that all the designers who emerged from Antwerp work from a purely Belgian perspective.

'I think if you compare it to the cinema, you find young British and Irish film-makers making good films for people in those countries. They could never make the same pictures if they went to Hollywood to work. Fashion designers in Paris make a different kind of garment, because in a big city you want to show yourself off. In Antwerp, you don't need clothes like that because people know you for *who* you are and not for *what* you are.'

The city is known for its classic tailoring and by a strange twist of fate Dries Van Noten's lofty and elegant Het Modepaleis faces another Van Noten store - originally owned by his grandfather.

As motorcycles go, Harley Davidsons don't count for much by modern standards but as noisy barometers of an affluent youth culture, they're hard to beat.

They are a sign that image rules supreme, and as you might expect, south Antwerp is awash with them; I counted 20 in one single hour outside ASA (another of Antwerp's fashionable drinking haunts). The people who ride them live in warehouse apartments, formerly the homes of immigrant dock workers. Bought for a song in the Fifties and Sixties, today they change hands for a million Belgian Francs.

Architect Peter Vermeulen is a typical new southerner. In the Eighties he and some friends bought a derelict fish-smoking factory which they have sensitively and ingeniously converted into six family homes. As it is a listed building, they have retained much of its original charm, including some of the smoking towers, and with them the pungent aroma.

'When we bought this building there was absolutely nothing in the whole south,' explains Vermeulen, a tall man with tousled hair. He wears those earthy, telluric shades of wool and linen favoured by so many inhabitants of this city. His family are eating lunch on the veranda overlooking a small courtyard, and through an arch two rabbits are napping in their hutch. This is modern urban living in the post-industrial age at its best.

'Two accidents brought new life to this area,' Vermeulen explains. 'The first was the arrival of the Museum of Modern Art here, and the second was the Photographic Museum. They weren't part of a strategic plan but they brought new people into an area that has many appealing intrinsic qualities: good architecture, good houses and wide streets. As these people bought in, property prices went up.'

Vermeulen's own house is in the former stables. A single space is divided into habitable compartments using a suspended floor and glass stairs to channel light. The entire project took 10 years from concept to moving in.

One of my favourites places is Cafe Beveren, on Zand, close to the river. Here sailors, whores, students, philosophers and drunken Dutchmen feed coins into the art deco 'Decap' jukebox on the back wall.

Too civilised, too old, too refined, too dignified
and nowadays, much, much too cool...

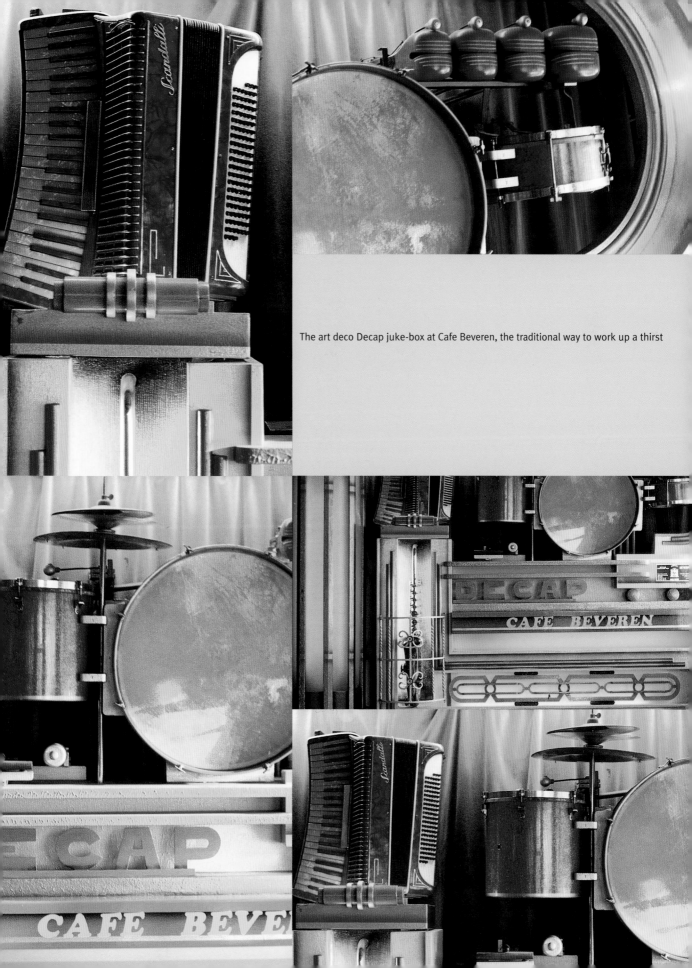

The art deco Decap juke-box at Cafe Beveren, the traditional way to work up a thirst

This is a contraption that looks like a Thirties ocean liner with drums, a saxophone, an accordion and percussion. The music it pumps out isn't any good for dancing, and it's hard to talk above it, but the locals love it and you will, too, once you have a couple of strong, dark, Belgian brews inside you.

It's in bars like this, Bar Tabac and Entrepôt du Congo, and in scores of others, that you'll find the new Antwerp. You can glimpse snapshots of history through the paintings of Rubens and Van Dyck, but if you want to feel the pulse of the city you've got to come to places like these.

Like the diamonds you hear about but seldom see, you have to know where to look (and where to drink) for Antwerp's gems.

Dock's Café
(right and page 113),
a post-modernist
berth to enjoy classic
Belgian cheese
served with Port

Cobh
Ballycotton
Kinsale
Bantry Bay
Dingle
Ring
of Kerry
Galway

An Irish scholar, asked
if there was a word in
Gaelic to correspond with
'mañana', considered
his reply carefully.
'We may', he finally replied,
'have some words that
are similar in meaning, but
nothing, nothing,
that conveys the dramatic
urgency of *mañana*'.

To appreciate fully the rugged and often spectacular coastline that stretches from Cobh in the south west of Ireland around to Galway, the main city of the west, it is advisable not to hurry. This is an area of Ireland rich in history and folklore, a culture that has withstood famine and emigration, invasion and occupation, and still defies the homogeneous tendencies and clock-watching mentality of the modern world. It is a land of narrow, winding cliff-top roads, hedgerows ignited with wild fuchsia, meandering between fields divided by old stone walls, before descending to tiny fishing villages and colourful ports. It is a land that has inspired writers and poets, musicians and artists, and today welcomes increasing numbers of visitors to share its beauty and relaxed way of life.

If Ireland today is as unspoilt as any country in Europe, it is largely as a result of the constant tide of emigration that began during the Great Famine of the 1840s, and which, to some degree, persists to this day. Nowhere is evidence of this more poignantly captured than in Cobh, which was Ireland's major port for much of this period, and is the start of our journey. Cobh was where most of those fleeing the famine embarked on the often perilous passage to the New World. In later times, its harbour (the second biggest natural harbour in the world), was home to many of the major liner companies. Cunard was just one to have offices here, and the Queen Elizabeth II remains a frequent visitor.

Cobh (left and right), today, is a pleasant mixture of graceful harbour frontages, Georgian crescents and steeply rising hillside homes. It is acutely conscious of its place in Irish history, having an imposing cathedral built with funds sent back by homesick emigrants, and a Heritage Centre, detailing its long, seafaring history, fashioned from an old railway station. Many famine emigrants escaped the ravages of the potato blight only to perish with fever on the 'coffin ships' taking them to America, and visitors can see the cramped conditions in the replicas of cabins

Sandeman
hot port

**A glass of Sandeman Port
slice of clove-studded lemon
brown sugar to taste
hot water**

Ask any Irish chef whom they credit with the renaissance of Irish cuisine, and the name of Myrtle Allen is likely to be top of the list.

from the old ships. They can read, too, about the heartache of the 'Emigrant's Wake', the last farewell to families and friends before setting off on the journey from which few returned. Tragedy was not limited to the famine era either, Cobh was the last port of call for the Titanic, and, in 1915, the Lusitania was sailing for the port when it was sunk.

For a more convivial appreciation of Cobh's naval heritage there can be no better place than Mansworth's, one of Ireland's most unspoilt pubs, and a meeting point for visiting sailors, captains and even admirals for more than 100 years. With its wooden floors and many original fittings, the pub's nautical character is enhanced with a remarkable collection of caps donated by visiting ships' crews over the years. And if there is anything you need to know about the history of Cobh, look no further than the landlord, John Mansworth, a sailing enthusiast and a direct descendant of the pub's original owner. On any evening at Mansworth's you might meet foreign sailors, a politician or media celebrity, and some of the local characters who give the pub its charm. Timothy Hayes, now in his sixties, won international fame in the 1960s with a world record for 101 hours buried underground. Timothy's feat is captured on film at the Heritage Centre, and just in case you fail to appreciate the enormity of his achievement, Timothy is often on hand to put you right.

The Irish, it has occasionally been noted, are fond of their drink, and Port, in its various forms, has long been a particular favourite. Traditionally, to ask for a glass of wine in an Irish pub meant a glass of Port, and a glass of Port in Ireland has always meant Sandeman's. In recent times, the centuries-old custom of drinking mulled Port in the cold winter months has been revived in the form of a hot Port toddy. Each pub has its own variation, but you could do worse than sample John Mansworth's version - Sandeman's Five Star with a slice of clove-studded lemon, brown sugar and hot water. For an unsettled stomach, Mansworth recommends 'Monkey's Blood' - half

Port, half brandy - but, as he observes, few locals bother waiting for a tummy ache.

At Ballymaloe House, near the little fishing village of Ballycotton, 26 miles from Cobh, another Irish tradition is also faithfully observed: the enjoyment of good food. Ask any top Irish chef whom they credit with the renaissance of Irish cuisine and the name of Myrtle Allen is likely to be top of the list. In 1964, Myrtle and her husband Ivan opened a restaurant at their beautifully restored Georgian house which is set in acres of farmland. At the time, Irish cuisine was in the doldrums, but with her use of good local produce and imaginative blend of the best in traditional Irish and international cooking, Myrtle soon won widespread acclaim. She has recently retired as head chef but continues to supervise the family in their running of the renowned cookery school, a thriving craft shop and produce business, as well as the hotel and restaurant.

On Sunday evening, as usual, the Allens all congregate around a large table in the restaurant and catch up on the week's events. Ivan sees to the wine and concludes the evening with a glass of his favourite 20-Year-Old Port. One by one Myrtle and Ivan are joined by their six children, who help run the business, as well as head chef Rory O'Connell, formerly of London's Chez Nico, and his sister, Darina Allen, herself a renowned cook, who runs the internationally acclaimed Ballymaloe Cookery School, close by in Midleton, with her husband and the eldest Allen son, Timothy.

The next morning Myrtle is up early to prepare her own contribution to this book, Port and Loganberry Jelly. She bustles through the busy but unusually good-natured kitchen, explaining, like all good chefs, that quantities are a matter of instinct and improvisation rather than facts and figures, before crowning her creation with rose petals from their extensive flower and vegetable gardens. Despite her recent retirement as head chef, Myrtle remains as busy as ever in her position as president

Port & loganberry jelly

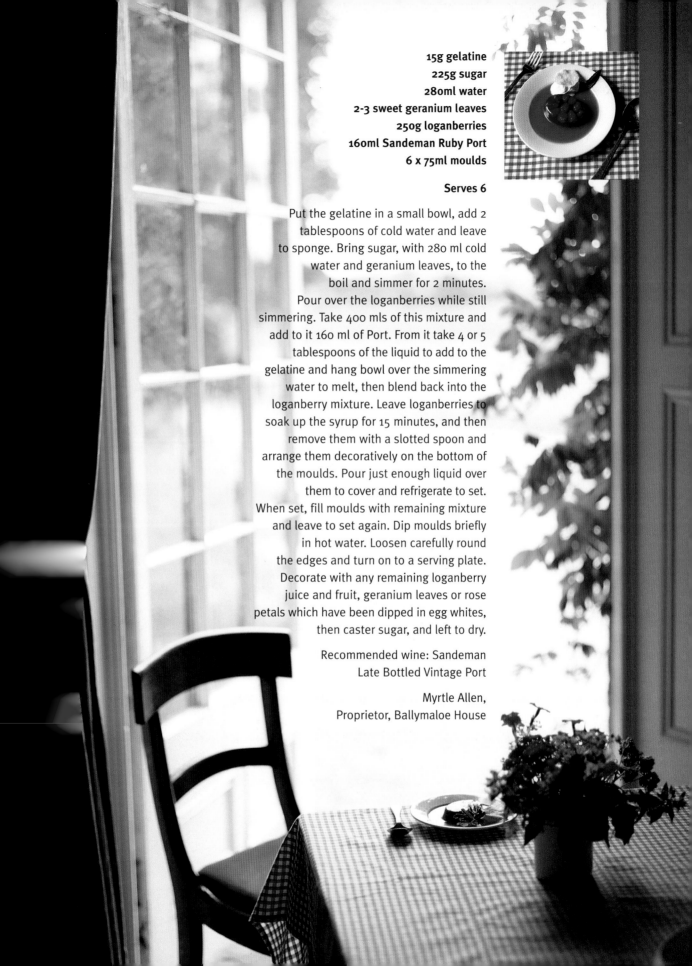

15g gelatine
225g sugar
280ml water
2-3 sweet geranium leaves
250g loganberries
160ml Sandeman Ruby Port
6 x 75ml moulds

Serves 6

Put the gelatine in a small bowl, add 2
tablespoons of cold water and leave
to sponge. Bring sugar, with 280 ml cold
water and geranium leaves, to the
boil and simmer for 2 minutes.
Pour over the loganberries while still
simmering. Take 400 mls of this mixture and
add to it 160 ml of Port. From it take 4 or 5
tablespoons of the liquid to add to the
gelatine and hang bowl over the simmering
water to melt, then blend back into the
loganberry mixture. Leave loganberries to
soak up the syrup for 15 minutes, and then
remove them with a slotted spoon and
arrange them decoratively on the bottom of
the moulds. Pour just enough liquid over
them to cover and refrigerate to set.
When set, fill moulds with remaining mixture
and leave to set again. Dip moulds briefly
in hot water. Loosen carefully round
the edges and turn on to a serving plate.
Decorate with any remaining loganberry
juice and fruit, geranium leaves or rose
petals which have been dipped in egg whites,
then caster sugar, and left to dry.

Recommended wine: Sandeman
Late Bottled Vintage Port

Myrtle Allen,
Proprietor, Ballymaloe House

Above and right: the beautifully restored
buildings and gardens of Ballymaloe House

of Euro-Toques, a European union of chefs formed to protect the rights of small and traditional food producers against the might of the European conglomerates and factory farmers. That this crusade has borne fruit, is evident at our next port of call.

Kinsale, a hilly fishing village, 18 miles southwest of Cork City, is known as the gourmet capital of Ireland, an accolade celebrated in the annual October Food Festival. Brian Cronin, the owner of the Blue Haven Hotel, is the only original member of The Good Food Circle, formed in the Seventies to put Kinsale on the food map. The Circle is a collection of local restaurateurs who agreed to pool their resources and work together to promote Kinsale. Like Myrtle Allen, whom he greatly admires, Cronin is a great believer in encouraging the use of local produce, and believes now is an exciting time for Irish cooking.

'We are creating an Irish cuisine, bringing back skills and experience from abroad and marrying them to ingredients grown here. We're still feeling our way, as Irish taste tends to the conservative, but we're taking new ideas on board and putting our own slant on good Irish produce.'

It is with good reason that the town is known as the medieval wine port of Kinsale. Sample a bottle of Château de Tracy Pouilly Fumé at the Blue Haven, and ask Cronin to explain the history of the 'Wine Geese.' These were largely wine merchants, some of the 'Wild Geese' (Irishmen forced to flee the country after three separate defeats at the hands of the English in the 17th century), who took up residence in France, Spain, Portugal and even in the New World, and set up wineries there. They were particularly influential in Bordeaux where the Châteaux of Lynch-Bages, Clarke, Lawton, McCartney, Kirwan and Phelan are still prominent. However, according to the distinguished Cork wine historian, Ted Murphy, the Irish relationship with wine goes back a great deal further – to prehistoric times, in fact, when it would have been bartered for jewellery.

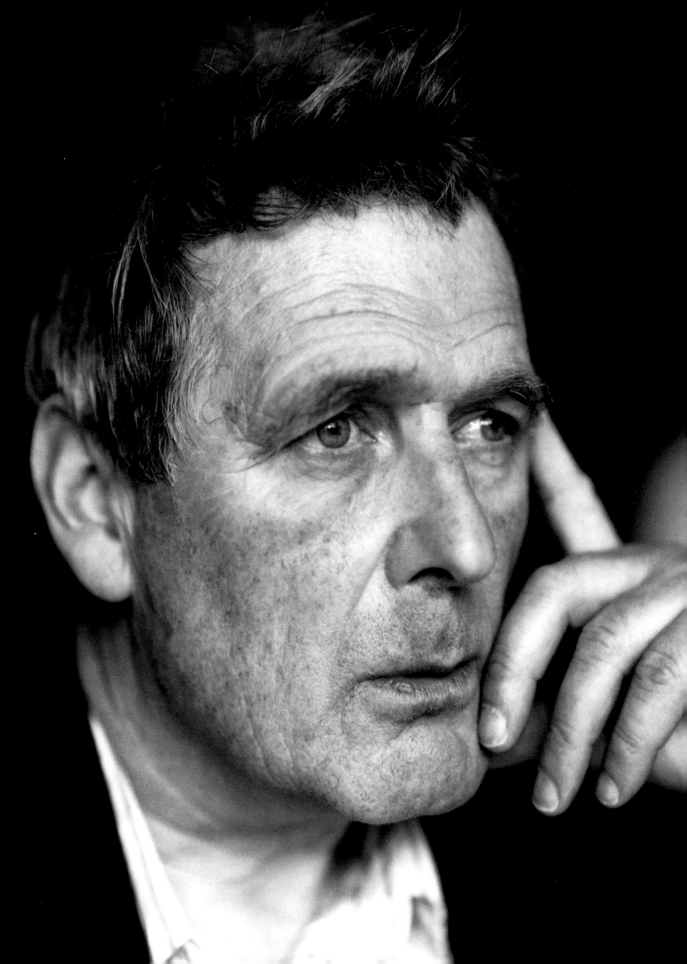

'In 433AD, St Patrick himself went to the hill of Tara and found the High Kings of Ireland drinking Gaulish wine, and, of course, with Christianity and the requirement of wine for mass, there was a great impetus for the wine trade here. By the end of the 18th century, Ireland was consuming four times as much wine as England, claret being the favourite drink, followed by Port. An indication of Port's enduring popularity here can be found in the records for March, 1903, of Cork wine merchants, Woodford Bourne, who bottled 4,300 bottles of Sandeman's Port in that month alone (until the early Fifties, Port was shipped into Ireland in pipes, and bottled locally). Considering that this was one wine merchant out of eight in a small city, it gives you a measure of the Irish penchant for Port!'

Much of the wine was smuggled into Ireland to avoid prohibitive taxes, usually to be bartered for wool. Kinsale was one of only 16 Irish ports officially designated to receive wine, and boasts its own smuggling caves, so it seems entirely fitting that Ireland's first Wine Museum, built to celebrate the Wine Geese, is to be housed in Desmond Castle, for many years the Customs House of Kinsale.

The legacy of Britain, both in terms of its occupation and the class of landed Irish Gentry which traces its roots back to England (the Anglo-Irish), is much in evidence in Cork, in the many Georgian houses of its towns and the occasional castles and stately homes dotted around its countryside. The coastal route from Kinsale around to Bantry, our next stop, reveals much evidence of the Anglo-Irish influence, particularly in Castletownshend, where two of their most illustrious authors, the cousins Edith Somerville and Violet Martin (writing under the pseudonym Martin Ross) created their famous novels.

Bantry itself has a long association with the days of British rule. The most commanding view of its beautiful bay is from the steps of the Italianate gardens of one of Ireland's most interesting stately homes, Bantry House. In 1796, the Irish nationalist, Wolfe Tone,

persuaded the French to launch an invasion of Ireland through Bantry Bay. A local landowner, Richard White, organised a Bantry militia to defend the town and allowed a British garrison to use his house. In the event, the French Armada turned back due to stormy weather, but White, the landlord of Bantry House, was granted an Earlship by a grateful George 111.

Bantry House, which, in 1945, became the first Irish stately home to be opened to the public, is run today by a descendant of the first Earl of Bantry, Egerton Shelswell-White. Although he sees himself primarily as a Bantry man, Shelswell-White is very much of Anglo-Irish stock, a charming and courteous host with a pronounced English accent and an enthusiasm for brass brand music (he plays trombone at the weekly gatherings of the local brass band at Bantry House). There is, though, a very relaxed Irish flavour to the house, with visitors trusted to wander unsupervised among the French tapestries, antique china, silver and the splendid family portraits. The distinctive portrait of George 111, a copy of a Ramsay original, was a gift to the family from the King himself.

Shelswell-White, educated at Winchester public school in England, was a history teacher in America for many years. He was raising horses in Arizona just before returning to take over stewardship of Bantry House after the death of his mother in the late Seventies. Since then he has devoted his time to a detailed and costly restoration of the house.

From Bantry Bay westwards, the scenery along the coastal route seems to get ever more wild and magnificent. From the Beara peninsula, jutting into the Atlantic, we drive around the precariously steep and narrow roads of the Ring of Kerry, overlooking waves crashing on to jagged cliffs, to the Dingle Peninsula. A few miles west of the fishing village of Dingle is a setting familiar to film buffs, the location for *Ryan's Daughter*. The village was destroyed once filming was over, but the old school remains, now no more than a shed with Atlantic views. The famous

Kruger's Bar nearby has been a favourite with the Irish literati for many years. Locals still remember helping build the village and sharing a drink or three with the cast here after shooting. The area has seen nothing like it for employment, before or since. 'In fact,' says one, a night-watchman on the set, 'it's a bloody shame Ryan hadn't another daughter or two!'

If ever there was scenery to inspire a writer, Kerry has it, and if ever there was a writer to do justice to Kerry, it is John B Keane, author of many novels, short stories and plays. The most renowned of these is *The Field*, later made into a successful film starring Richard Harris. Keane sits in the tiny pub that bears his name in the market town of Listowel, and in the melodic dialect of the Kerry countrymen, whose culture and history form the backbone of his work, Keane pays tribute to the qualities of the landscape around him.

'The gigantic features of the coastline; the beauty of its lakes, serenity of its coves and balmy glades... There is a sense of place here, a fierce awareness of earth and water and wind and rain, an overpowering affinity with these elements. When I am away, I miss, most of all, the music of the river. The moods and tunes of a river are changing forever just like ourselves – there is nothing reliable about the river and nothing reliable about ourselves. I am a natural part of all this and it is the best part of my life.'

Leaving the town as a boy to live with his 'country cousins', Keane found his pathway into drama through the clash of cultures, delighting in the traditions of the country people and in the richness and colour of their language. Now he sees himself as their true representative. Central to his work is the deeply ingrained relationship between the Irish and their land, a theme most powerfully evoked in *The Field*.

'*The Field* is about what land meant to people. Since the advent of landlordism, when the Irish lost their land to the Scots in the North and English in the South, it has been the desire of every Irishman, until recent times, to own his own piece of land.

'Like all the Sandemans, my great-grand uncle Fleetwood enjoyed a special relationship with Ireland and with wine. A noted *bon viveur*, he once disappeared for some time during a business trip in Ireland. Frantic efforts were made to locate him, but to no avail. Finally, Sandeman in London received a desperate call from an Irish hotelier: would they please come and collect their brother as he had taken root in their cellar and was rapidly consuming their entire stock of Vintage wine.

George Sandeman

'The gigantic features of the coastline;
the beauty of its lakes,
serenity of its coves and balmy glades
...there is a sense of place here,
a fierce awareness of earth and water
and wind and rain, an overpowering
affinity with these elements.
When I am away I miss, most of all,
the music of the river. The moods and
tunes of a river are changing forever,
just like ourselves - there is
nothing reliable about the river and
nothing reliable about ourselves.
I am a natural part of all this and it is
the best part of my life.' John B Keane

Every field had a special significance for a family, each field had a name: 'Aristotle', 'The Arguing Field'...That little piece of land, that legacy, is the source of all I am. And we survived war, plagues, famine, everything with that land. It's a love affair!'

The Kerry countryside and its people are entwined in Keane's work, his characters as vivid and expressive as the land they inhabit. 'It is because I come from melodramatic countryside,' Keane explains. 'Our every pronouncement is melodramatic because of the ritual that surrounds it, and I am infused by its colour.' The enjoyment of drink has always been part of the closely knit social life of the country people, and as a chronicler of country customs, and a publican as well as a writer, Keane often makes reference in his work to the Irish countrywomen's fondness for Port, as this excerpt from his acclaimed novel, *The Bodhran Makers*, testifies.
' "Come on," Delia Bluenose taunted her husband. "Pull on a pair of these and I'll show you how to box". She threw a pair of gloves at his feet and drew on the other pair before standing upright and shaping like a boxer. "Sit down you foolish oul' woman", Bluenose advised her. "Come on you coward", she called, fortified by the best part of a bottle of Sandeman's Five Star.'

From Keane's Kerry we drive into Clare to see the magnificent cliffs of Moher, high above the Atlantic, and distant views of the Aran Islands. The British influence is sparse here and Irish is often the first language of the 'Westerners'. Irish music, too, has its strongholds here, such as the fishing village of Doolin where, most evenings, the pubs are alive with the sound of the bodhran(a percussion instrument) and the fiddle. From here we go north through the stony, prehistoric scenery of the Burren to Moran's Oyster Cottage (opposite), situated on a weir, in an inlet of Galway Bay.

Oysters used to be the poor man's food, and during the Irish Famine they kept thousands of coastal dwellers from starvation. Today, Irish oysters are a favoured delicacy, and Willie Moran welcomes visitors from all over the world to the bar that has been in his family for seven generations. The Cottage has attracted its fair share of celebrities: Roger Moore, Pierce Brosnan, Paul Newman and the Emperor and Empress of Japan, and was even celebrated in verse by Noël Coward. But as this is Ireland, don't be surprised to find a lorry driver and millionaire sharing a dozen oysters, washed down with a Guinness or Willie Moran's recommendation, a glass of dry, White Port.

'The tradition of Port and oysters goes back to the days of the Anglo-Irish gentry, when a great deal of fish and seafood were eaten.' Moran explains. 'Port became a popular accompaniment to oysters because, unlike whiskey, it doesn't harden the stomach. These things go in cycles, and now the young people are developing a taste for oysters again, and with it a taste for Port.'

Whether its the salmon caught in the gable of the old water mill nearby, crab, mussels or oysters, all the seafood here is fresh and local. Willie (holder of the world record for oyster opening – 91 seconds to open and present 30 oysters) has no doubt that the Edlus oyster he serves from September to April, from a 700-acre bed at the mouth of a nearby river, is the best in the world. 'Good oysters,' Willie insists, 'must have a salty flavour, a balance of the sea and the river.' Enjoy them with a glass of dry, White Port, finish the evening with an Irish whiskey or two, and, who knows, you may be as lucky as Noël Coward in his tribute to Moran's:

'After all these oysters
and the whiskies you have drunk here,
you also might see mermaids
gently swimming in the weir.'

'After all these oysters
and the whiskies you have drunk here,
you also might see mermaids
gently swimming in the weir.'

Noël Coward

New York

There's a telling scene in Martin Scorsese's New York gangster epic *Goodfellas*, in which a standup comedian tells the story about his wife's birthday. As a gift he offers her a trip – anywhere, to which she replies 'How about somewhere I've never been before?' And he says, 'OK, how about the kitchen?'

As far as New Yorkers are concerned, cooking is something accountants do to avoid paying federal tax. Half of them don't have kitchens and the other half simply aren't interested. In the Big Apple food should be consumed in public – in one of Manhattan's 15,000 restaurants.

Brian McNally, President of restaurant "44" in The Royalton hotel (pictured left and right), puts New Yorkers' eating out habits into perspective: 'Nobody in New York can bear to stay at home. Here, the domestic dinner is dead, because most people who live here are ferociously ambitious. They're not here to stay at home, they're here to make money!'

Naturally, along with the New Yorker's extensive knowledge of fine food is an understanding and appreciation of wine and liquor. In keeping with New York's mix-it-up attitude, how and where Port is served – uptown or downtown – is as changeable as the people, the architecture, and the lifestyles of each neighbourhood.

The Upper East Side has long been the home of the city's high society socialites, European jet-setters, CEOs, and everyone from Woody Allen to the late Jackie O have occupied the penthouse apartments along Fifth and Park Avenues. Cultural icons, such as the Metropolitan, Whitney, Frick and Guggenheim museums line Fifth Avenue, and the shopping on Madison Avenue is comparable to the Avenue Montaigne in Paris. It is also home to one of the city's most acclaimed restaurants, Daniel. Daniel opened on the quiet, tree-lined 76th Street, between Fifth Avenue and Madison Avenue, when Daniel Boulud, in what some considered a scandalous move, left his position as head chef at the illustrious, four-star restaurant, Le Cirque, to establish his own

'Nobody in New York can bear to stay
at home. Here, the domestic dinner is
dead, because most people who live
here are ferociously ambitious. They
are not here to stay at home, they are
here to make money!'

Brian McNally

place. Now, even the most sceptical critics agree Boulud made the right move. Although he was trained in the tradition of classic French restaurants, Boulud's latest venture differs in its relaxed atmosphere and in a menu that culls flavours and ingredients from around the world. Port wine often features in Boulud's creations, whether it's a Pepper Tuna with Parsnip Purée and a Shallot Confit with Port sauce, or a terrine of *foie gras*, or a reduced Port glaze sauce that goes well with several types of fish. 'I like the deep flavour of Port when it's reduced as a sauce, because it has a sweet-sour note,' says Boulud. When it comes to dessert, he often serves figs, blackberries or pears with Port.

Heading towards mid-town, down Fifth Avenue past Tiffany, Gucci, Bulgari, and other tiny boutiques, is a restaurant which epitomises old New York, the '21' Club. Walking past the cast-iron jockeys outside the front door at 21 East 52nd Street, and into the low-ceilinged, dark interior of the '21' Club, it is easy to imagine its more raucous days as one of New York's swank speak-easies, a place where the famous and the infamous always felt at home, ate well, and drank even better. From the ceiling downstairs hangs a hodge-podge of memorabilia, most donated by customers. An autographed football and a miniature truck of an oil magnate's company, are among the many permanent emblems of the wealth and talent that have walked through the club's doors. Today, the "21" Club is a favourite lunch spot for several media moguls, such as Revlon's Ronald Perleman, Mirabella's Grace Mirabella, and ABC's Diane Sawyer. Here, the consumption of Port is well above average for New York restaurants. 'In New York, Port is still considered a beverage of the rich and famous,' says Christopher Shipley, the beverage manager, 'Port has a certain cachet here, and our customers treat it as a special event beverage.' Interested in seeing their stock? Ask the bartender to take you on a tour of the wine cellar. You'll pass through the kitchen and walk down a brick-walled corridor. The invisible entrance to the cellar is a crack in the wall, which opens when a long wire 'key', much like a coat hanger, is inserted. Suddenly you're standing in a cavernous, dark cellar. Here some of '21''s best customers have kept private wine bins (Richard Nixon's is still full) There is also a private dining room, bathed in red light (it was once part of the speak-easy), where customers can hold private parties. 'Several of our customers keep Port in our cellar,' says Shipley. 'In fact, traditionally, when our customers have children, they put some down to open up when they turn 21, since we are the '21' club.' Shipley keeps the bar stocked with several Vintages dating back to 1963, which are available by the glass, and rare bottles dating back as far as 1945. 'People who come here expect to get the best Vintage of the century. We have it.'

Another bastion of New York's classic bar/restaurants is on the 65th floor of 30 Rockefeller Plaza. First opened in 1934, the Rainbow Room was conceived by John D Rockefeller as the finishing touch to his landmark building. When it opened it was a cocktail lounge and restaurant which offered big band entertainment. (Rumour has it Fred and Ginger danced here.) Today, its original art deco interior has been restored and it still has some of the best cabaret talent in the city, as well as a breathtaking view of the skyline. 'We're noted for our classic cocktails,' says Dale DeGroff, the Rainbow Room's beverage manager and veteran bartender, who is known for his coffee cocktail, a port-based recipe from the 19th century. DeGroff was taught how to make it by a previous owner of the Rainbow Room, who learned the recipe from the speak-easies he worked in in the 1920s. Easy to make, the cocktail is equal parts Port and brandy, (you can use Tawny or Ruby—DeGroff prefers Ruby), an egg yolk, and a teaspoon of sugar. DeGroff notes that because eggs are larger today, little more than half a yolk is needed. The ingredients are then shaken vigorously until they emulsify. The result: a delicious drink that resembles coffee with cream.

Peppered tuna with parsnip purée & shallot confit in port wine

For the Shallot Confit:
1 cup of very finely chopped shallots
2 cups of Sandeman Ruby Port
2 cups of red wine
2 stems thyme

For the Purée:
3 cups of peeled parsnips cut into 1cm cubes
1 cup of potatoes peeled and cut into 2.5cm cubes
1 cup of milk and 1/2 cup of double cream

For the Sauce:
2 tbsp of olive oil
1/2 cup tuna scraps or fish bones
1/2 cup minced shallots
1 stem of thyme
1 cup of Sandeman Ruby Port, 1 cup of red wine
2 cups of veal or beef jus or stock
1 tbsp of butter
4 tuna steaks 2.5cm thick (about 200g each)
salt and 1 tbsp of crushed black pepper
fresh chives cut into 15cm strips

Serves 4

Shallot confit: In a small casserole over a low heat, add the shallots, 2 cups Port, 2 cups red wine, thyme and let simmer slowly until the liquid is mostly evaporated (about 1 1/2 hours). Set aside to cool.

Parsnip purée: While the shallots are cooking, in a separate casserole add the parsnips, potatoes and a touch of salt. Bring to the boil and let simmer until the parsnips are very tender. Drain. Heat the milk and cream together. Press the parsnips and potatoes through a fine mesh. Sift, then whip in the milk, a little at a time, until you get a light and fluffy purée. Add seasoning and keep warm aside.

Sauce: In a low casserole over a medium heat, add 1 tbsp of olive oil, the fish bones, shallots and thyme. Sweat 5-8 minutes, pour over the wine and Port, let boil and reduce to a glaze. Add the stock and simmer for 10-15 minutes or until you obtain 3/4 cup of sauce. Skim the surface of the sauce often. While reducing, finish the sauce by whipping 1 tbsp of butter, season to taste and keep warm aside.

In a very hot pan over a high heat add 1 tbsp of olive oil. Season the tuna steak with salt and black pepper. Sear both sides very quickly (about 3 minutes each side for rare). When cooked, remove and cut the tuna in 1.5cm strips. Arrange a dome of purée in the centre of the plate, place a spoon of the shallot confit over it and then place the the strips of tuna on top. To finish, drizzle the sauce around the plate.

Garnish with thin slices of baked parsnip and fresh chives.

Recommended wine: Crozes Hermitage 1993

Daniel Boulud, Chef/Proprietor, Daniel

The Rainbow Room also serves several Ports by the glass, especially a '63 that DeGroff keeps on hand for some clients who come during the day, when the Rainbow Room becomes the Rockefeller Club, for private members.

'Americans haven't been brought up on Port like the British, but the interest has been growing steadily over the past decade', says Peter Morrell, chairman of Morrell Wine and Spirits Merchants, which stocks the wine cellars of several Park Avenue residences. 'Port is the most fascinating wine known to man', Morrell continues, 'because it can age almost forever and develops incredible aromas and flavours.'

While New Yorkers pride themselves on their more European ways, one European tradition that hasn't totally caught on is drinking Port as an aperitif. 'Everyone in America wants Vintage Ports, unlike Portugal and France where they drink Tawny and Ruby before dinner', says Michael Yurch, the executive vice-president of Sherry Lehman, New York's world-renowned wine and liquor store on Madison Avenue. 'In America, the aperitif is a lost art. Here, it's thought of as an age-worthy ritualistic dessert wine, served often after a big feast with cigars. Of course, New Yorkers, compared with other Americans, are rather more sophisticated about Vintage Port.'

A trip down to Greenwich Village still conjures up visions of past decades. Beat poets pounding bongos and reciting haikus in dusty speak-easies left over from the Thirties. Bob Dylan, Allen Ginsberg, William Burroughs roaming Bleeker Street and its alleyways in the Sixties, and Andy Warhol, singer Patti Smith and photographer Robert Mapplethorpe hanging out near Union Square in the Seventies. Downtown New York has always lived by its own rules.

Downtown sophistication has an edge. While its restaurants may lack in tradition compared with restaurants and bars uptown, they make up for it with their inventive cuisine and laidback style. In the middle of the Village, on East 12th Street, is the Gotham Bar & Grill, a restaurant that opened in 1984 and quickly became a favourite stomping ground for New York's hip young professionals, where artists rub shoulders with investment bankers. While New Yorkers are always in search of a scene, they come here for chef Alfred Portale's unusual dishes and outrageous sense of display. Even the most jaded are awed by his vertical, gravity-defying creations that resemble the skyscraper skyline just outside. One of the restaurant's most popular entrées is Portale's Wild-Striped Bass with Port. His wine list, with more than 220 selections, is just as impressive. 'People are fascinated with vintage Port', says Portale. 'We serve several half-bottles that are perfect for small parties. If someone wants to know what food will go best with our Ports, we are glad to tell them, but I don't believe in matching food with drink, if someone wants a Chardonnay with their steak, it's okay with me'.

At first glance, Montrachet resembles a French bistro with its antique-style bar at the front groaning under the weight of hundreds of bottles of wine. Once inside, it is more in keeping with the decor and style of Californian *nouvelle cuisine*. Located in the hyper-hip downtown area called Tribeca (home to such artists and actors as Harvey Keitel, Robert DeNiro and Christopher Walken), Montrachet is a wine connoisseur's heaven, and Wall Street's finest can be seen here winding down from work, alongside other high-rollers who come for the relaxed, unpretentious atmosphere. Eavesdrop on other tables' conversations, and you're likely to hear intense discussion about the wine being served or a recent case bought at auction. Montrachet is a restaurant where the wine doesn't just complement the meal, it's the highlight. So it's not surprising that Daniel Johnnes, the wine director, prefers to serve Port by itself after a meal. 'I like Port after dessert, so it doesn't compete with the sweetness of dessert.' Montrachet is also one of the few New York

coffee cocktail: port brandy egg yolk sugar

For the Rainbow Room's Coffee Cocktail: equal parts of Sandeman Ruby Port and brandy half an egg yolk teaspoon of sugar

Shake vigorously with ice in a cocktail mixer, pour through a strainer into a glass.

'**New York's** a small place when it comes to the part of it that wakes up just as the rest of it is going to bed.'   P G Wodehouse

6 x 200g black sea bass fillets (or red snapper)
2 tbsp olive oil
3 cups loosely packed Swiss chard
18 tiny young carrots
2 dozen small boiled yellow fin potatoes

For the sauce:
3 medium cloves garlic, finely minced
4 large shallots, finely minced
175g aged red wine vinegar
200ml Sandeman Ruby Port
75g double cream
275g butter
3 tbsp fresh minced chives
salt and fresh ground white pepper

Serves 6

Sautéed black sea bass with Swiss chard, baby carrots and yellow fin potatoes in a vintage port and red wine vinegar sauce

For the sauce: in a medium saucepan combine minced garlic, shallots, Port and vinegar. Reduce over a high heat until liquid reaches a syrupy consistency. Add double cream. Bring to boil and reduce slightly. Lower heat and over a low flame whisk in the butter, piece by piece, until all the butter is emulsified and the sauce is a creamy consistency. Strain and keep warm.

Steam Swiss chard until just tender. Separately, boil yellow fin potatoes and tiny young carrots until just tender. Assemble vegetables and keep warm.

Season sea bass with salt and pepper. Heat approximately 1 tbspn of olive oil in a heavy-bottomed sauté pan. Add seasoned fillets skin-side down, approximately 3 minutes each side, on a high heat. Fish should be nicely brown, a deep colour, yet moist in the centre. Mound a spoonful of vegetables in the center of each plate. Place the fish on top, allowing 1 fillet per person. Add 3 tspns of chives to the sauce and then spoon sauce around and over the fish.

Recommended wine: Liparita, Californian Merlot
Alfred Portale, Chef, Gotham Bar & Grill

Alfred Portale

restaurants that serves chilled Tawnies as aperitifs, and keeps several very complex Vintages that date back 20 -30 years. 'In the end Port is a classic drink,' says Johnnes, 'and classics are always the best.'

While Port has always been an age-old standard among the finest restaurants, it is also being enjoyed by a newer generation in neo-traditional ways. New Yorkers love to go out, but after the glitz and gluttony of the Eighties, New Yorkers swore off extravagant galas and dancing at clubs till dawn, vowing to keep quiet, keep their cash, and stay at home. It didn't last long. But what has replaced the brashness of the Eighties is a more elegant, subdued form of going out, in which the bar has shifted back into focus; not the raucous, rowdy kind, but more sophisticated, quiet venues. As Mark Grossich said in *The New York Times* recently: 'The club scene was kind of fading away. People wanted to return to intimacy. People wanted a place to talk.' His solution: a trio of bars called Bar and Books, which he recently opened on Lexington Avenue at 73rd Street, downtown on Hudson Street, and midtown at Beekman Place, which is also connected to The Cigar Bar. These library-styled bars with books to read while sipping a glass of Port, are super hip with a literary tilt. But part of the reason for their sudden popularity is a resurgence of cigar smoking in New York. Today, Grossich's bars are some of the very few places a man or woman can enjoy a cigar with a cocktail. And over the past year, cigar parties, or tastings, have become the rage, especially for the younger set for whom smoking a cigar and sipping a glass of Port or whisky is a new experience. Marvin Shanken, editor-in-chief of *The Wine Spectator* (the American wine industry's bible), recently launched the magazine *Cigar Aficionado*, which is largely responsible for this renaissance in cigar appreciation. (Mr. Shanken is also an avid collector of Port). Cigar tastings are now held each month in New York at such places as the Bar and Books bars. Grossich recently started a cigar night for young women professionals at Alfred

Opposite: the bathroom at the Paramount hotel.
This page: Philippe Starck's trademark designs

Dunhill on 57th Street, which was extremely successful. 'The cigar is an appropriate companion to a glass of Port,' says Grossich.' Their sweetness in taste are very compatible.'

In precisely the same way that Neanderthal man lost his webbed feet and grew toes when he abandoned the sea and set off upon *terra firma,* so New Yorkers have dispensed with kitchens and, through necessity, evolved an insatiable appetite for dining out at restaurants and bars. And better still, while those space cadets on America's West Coast eschew the finer things in life in preference to a diet of leotards and mineral water, New Yorkers still cherish those icons of intimacy and style that have enriched our lives for centuries.

Kitchens – who needs 'em? Give me a Big Apple bar and a menu in a leather-bound, smoke-filled room any day. That's what I call a holiday.

Mark Grossich at Bar and Books

'The club scene was kind of fading away. People wanted to return to intimacy. People wanted a place to talk.'

Chef's choice

New York's top restaurateurs select their favourite combinations of Port and food

Oyster Bar

Grand Central Station, New York,
tel 212 490 6650

MARK ABRAHAMSON (General Manager): 'We serve nine Ports by the glass, from Tawny to Ruby to Vintage Reserves. Unlike people in European countries, our customers do not usually drink Port with oysters or any other type of seafood. Americans find Port too sweet for oysters. Usually, we serve it with dessert; chocolate desserts in particular. We have a bakery on the premises so we have different chocolate desserts available each day.'

Jo Jo

160 East 64th Street, New York,
tel 212 223 5656

PHILIPPE VONGERICHTEN (Maître d'): 'We mainly serve a Sandeman Founder's Reserve at our restaurant, and no vintage. We recommend a glass of it with our Valhrona Chocolate Cake that has a molten chocolate centre. We often use a Ruby Port sauce for our *Canard à l'Orange*. Another dessert it goes particularly well with is a Pastry of Autumn Fruits, dried figs, apple, and pears, with a blackcurrant juice, a honey cream glaze, and caramel ice cream.'

Gramercy Tavern

42 East 20th Street, New York,
tel 212 477 0777

BOB WENZI (Beverage Director): 'Port is a great richening agent to cook with, for figs, and also in savoury preparations. Our customers are big, big Port fans, and all our Ports, mainly Vintage (some dating back to 1906), are served by the glass. For anyone who has a cursory interest in Port, it's great to taste something from a special year that has a nostalgia or meaning to the customer. Tawnies are my favourite, because they're gentler and more versatile with food. They're also a wonderful introduction to Port, like Port with training wheels. We often offer white Port after a meal instead of Cognac. We often serve Ports with our cheeses, with our dozen-and-a-half-or-so farmstead cheeses, and a dozen Ports to choose from. It's a fun way to finish off a meal instead of going straight to dessert and coffee.'

Savoy

70 Prince Street (at Crosby), New York,
tel 212 219 8570

PETER HOFFMAN (Chef): 'We have served port for many years, either a true Vintage half bottle or non-Vintage Rubies by the glass. We usually serve port with a platter of nuts — chestnuts, filberts, brazil nuts, walnuts — in the shell on antique, grape-leaf trays with nut crackers, while our customers sit by the fire. It's not super-traditional, but the complete luxury of sitting by the fire gives an atmosphere of an English drawing room, and somehow the nuts fit well.'

Palm

837 Second Avenue, New York,
tel 212 687 2953

CHRIS GILMAN (Managing Director): 'Most of our Ports are served with dessert, but you can never let the dessert be sweeter than the Port, it destroys the flavour. Usually we serve it with something chocolate. Also, with cigars becoming popular, we have a designated smoking room where our customers can enjoy a glass of Port and a cigar. In fact, recently we had a wine and cigar dinner that finished off with Sandeman Port.'

Zoe

90 Prince Street, New York,
tel 212 966 6722

STEVEN LEFREDO (Owner): 'We are noted for our beverage programme, with a five page after-dinner drink list that includes eight types of Port, from the simplest Ruby to a 1966 Vintage. Here, Port is still seen as an after-dinner drink, even though, unlike Cognac, it can be consumed with food. At the moment, we are creating a specific dessert, a Fig and Cheese Tart, that will be available on the menu with a glass of Port. Of course, the modern American marriage is Port with a chocolate dessert.'

Matthew's

1030 Third Avenue, New York,
tel 212 838 4343

MATTHEW KENNEY (Chef /Owner): 'My favourite Port combination is when it is served with such Spanish cheeses as a *manchego cabalas*, a sort of *asiago*, and *queso tetilla*, a more mild, fontina-type cheese.
It's also very good with *foie gras*, because the buttery rich flavour of the *foie gras* lends itself to sweeter wines. I also cook a lot with Port: a Port wine flan, a reduction of Port dressing for a cold pheasant salad, and sauces for venison and duck. I have a
sweet tooth, so I prefer Vintage Port because it has a unique flavour.'

Union Square Cafe

21 East 16th Street, New York,
tel 212 243 4020

KAREN ANN KING (Wine Director): 'Our customers are inclined to order Vintage Ports, and we have them dating back to 1975, 1985, and on up. For those who are experimenting with Port, I usually suggest a 20-Year-Old Tawny, usually at the end of a meal in place of dessert. We can provide a cheese plate if asked, and often customers order Port with our pumpkin flan, but I prefer a glass of Port on its own.'

Le Bernardin

155 West 51st Street, New York,
tel 212 489 1515

RICHARD HOLLOCOU (General Manager): 'We do use Port in one recipe, our Red Snapper in a Port Wine Sauce and Cherry Vinegar. I would say 95% of our customers have Port by itself after their meal. We have more than a dozen Ports that date back as far as 1960, including a '63 and '77 by Sandeman. I find that most of our guests prefer Rubies, but as far as seasons are concerned, we sell just as much Port in summer as we do in winter.'

Circo

120 West 55th Street, New York,
tel 212 265 3636

MARCO MACCIONI (Co-owner): ' We serve five Ports by the glass including three Sandemans, which are Quinta do Vau, a Ruby and a Tawny. We serve quite a lot as aperitifs, as well as after dinner. At my father's restaurant, Le Cirque, they serve Port like it's
going out of style, and offer more than 20 different ones. At Circo, some of our patrons like to sit at the bar and drink it while having a good cigar. We also sauté several fresh fruits, such as figs, in Port for dessert, and we also use Port in entrées such as our Braised Veal Shank. Myself, I prefer a thicker Port, something to chew on such as Quinta do Vau. Vintage Ports are meatier, I like their spicey flavour, and especially those with a touch of vanilla.'

" 44 "

Royalton Hotel
44 West 44th Street, New York,
tel 212 944 8844

JAMES ROSENBAUER (Executive Chef): 'I would suggest our terrine of New York State *Foie Gras* with Roasted Quince and Port to be served with a Late Bottled Vintage Port because the richness and texture of the *foie gras* complements the rich flavour of the Port.'

Aureole

34 East 61st Street, New York,
tel 212 319 1660

VINCENT SANTORO (General Manager): 'We have eight Ports that we serve by the glass and by the bottle, from Vintage Tawnies to Vintage Characters. Our customers typically have a glass after their meal, usually with our cheese plate. We have a creamery upstate where we make all our cheeses — goat, sheep, and cow's milk cheeses. Then we serve the cheese with a Pear Terrine and Seasonal Figs. There is also a Cool Caramel Mousse, which is almost frozen, that goes well with Port.'

The Lobster Club

24 East 80th Street, New York,
tel 212 249 6500

ANNE ROSENZWEIG (Owner/Chef): 'One of the few unusual things we do when people order Port is to offer warm pistachios. I have a friend in the Napa Valley who introduced it to us. We do serve Ruby Port with our Warm Chocolate Bread pudding with a Port Custard Sauce. Personally, there are times when I want to have a great Vintage and other times when I want to have a Tawny. It's unfortunate that people think that you have to drink a Tawny in the summer and a heavier Vintage in the winter. Port is a wonderful way to round out a meal and make it last a little longer.'

port to port - cookery schools

ITALY

Regional Italy

The regional dishes from Piedmont, Tuscany, Sicily and Veneto are explored in a week of hands-on cooking classes (in English) and visits to local markets, to wine and olive oil tastings, and mushroom hunting expeditions. Accommodation is in family homes such as the 18th century *Palazzo* Ravida, in Sicily or a converted monastery in Piedmont. Courses are designed to appeal to people of all abilities from the enthusiastic amateur to the professional.

Tasting Italy, 97 Bravington Road, London W9 3AA, tel 0181 964 5839 fax 0181 960 3919.

Venice

The Hotel Cipriani has designed a series of cookery courses run by Giuliano Hazan and other internationally renowned cookery writers. Giuliano Hazan has taken over from his mother, Marcella Hazan, whose famous cookery classes were held for 16 years at her 16th century *palazzo* home. As well as practical lessons in the Cipriani, the courses will include visits to the kitchens of Venice's famous *palazzi* and restaurants, trips around the food markets, as well as olive oil , wine and cheese tastings.

Orient Express Hotels, tel 0181 568 8366, Hotel Cipriani, tel 00 39 41 5207744.

Orvieto

Renowned chef/restaurateur Alastair Little runs week-long courses at La Cacciata, a working farmhouse in the hills of Umbria. The emphasis is on using seasonal ingredients in local dishes that can be prepared at home. Classes include demonstrations as well as hands-on experience, and guest chefs include Antony Worrall Thompson, Sophie Braimbridge and Mauro Bregoli.

La Cacciata, Orvieto, Umbria, Italy
For information call or fax Sarah Robson,
tel 0181 675 9034.

FRANCE

Hampton House Travel offers cookery courses at two of their chateaux in Normandy and Provence. Taste of Calvados is held at the 18th Chateau du Tertre, near Caen, and Taste of Provence at the family-run Hostellerie Bérard, just outside Cassis. The four-day courses include visits to food markets and vineyards, shopping trips and food preparation.

Hampton House Travel,
tel 0181 871 3300 fax 0181 871 3322.

GREECE

Two seven-day courses run by Andy Harris, the author of *A Taste of the Aegean* (Picador), explore the traditional tastes of rural Greece from oven-baked stews to the celebratory dishes of Greek Easter. As well as practical experience in the kitchen, the course includes fishing trips, market visits and an invitation to eat in a Greek family home. The residential courses take place on the beautiful family estate of Candeli, in the village of Prokopi, on the unspoilt island of Evia.

Elysian Holidays, 14 Tower St, Rye,
East Sussex, TN31 7AT,
tel 01797 225482 fax 01797 225483.

Opposite page: Hotel Cipriani's Head Chef, Renato Piccolotto, tasting Grappa for the hotel's celebrated ice-cream dessert
Above: the beautiful gardens at Darina Allen's cookery school

ENGLAND

London

Leith's School of Food and Wine was established in 1975 by Prue Leith and Caroline Waldegrave, originally for those hoping to turn professional, but there are some holiday courses (beginners to advanced), for enthusiatic amateurs. Classes take place in London, and occasionally in Rhonda, Andalusia.

Leith's School of Food and Wine, 21 St Alban's Grove, London W8
tel 0171 229 0177.

London

Le Cordon Bleu Culinary Institute offers a variety of courses from evening classes to full-time diplomas, where you can learn everything from boulangerie and patisserie skills, to the dinner-party special – Entertaining with Style – and the classic Cordon Bleu Catering.

Le Cordon Bleu, L'Art Culinaire,114 Marylebone Lane, London W1,
tel 0171 935 3503 fax 0171 935 7621.

Somerset

Cookery at The Grange offers a range of courses in a converted 17th century coach house in the grounds of Whatley Vineyard, near Bath. Run by Jane and William Averill, The Grange specialises in the use of local produce such as fresh fish, cheese, butter and clotted cream, and herbs from their own garden. Courses run from weekend beginners' to the four-week Basics to Bearnaise for would-be professionals.

Cookery at the Grange, Whatley Vineyard, Frome, Somerset BA11 3LA,
tel 01373 836579.

Hertfordshire

As an antidote to the bland, meatless recipes of the Seventies, chef Roselyne Masselin came up with La Cuisine Imaginaire – her idea of vegetarian cooking for the Nineties. She now runs a school of the same name which caters for the glamorous, gourmet-dinner-party end of the veggie market.

Emphasis is on style, presentation and taste, and shows influences from the Middle East, the Mediterranean and Masselin's native Normandy. The courses cater for everyone from the total beginner to trainee superchefs.

La Cuisine Imaginaire, 18 Belmont Court, Belmont Hill, St Albans, Hertfordshire AL1 1RB,
tel 01727 837643 fax 01727 8476436.

EIRE

County Cork

Darina Allen teaches classic dishes such as Carrageen Moss Pudding, Colcannon and Dublin Coddle at the school she and her husband Tim have been running since 1983. The school is 10 minutes from the renowned Ballymaloe House hotel.

Ballymaloe Cookery School, Shanagarry, Midleton, County Cork, Ireland,
tel 00 353 21 64 67 85.

Literary Port

'Of all our venerable British of the two Isles professing a suckling attachment to an ancient Port wine, lawyer, doctor, squire, rosy admiral, city merchant, the classical scholar is he whose blood is most nuptial to the webbed bottle.... Port hymns to his conservativism. It is magical: at one sip he is off swimming in the purple flood of the ever-youthful antique.'
George Meredith, *The Egotist*

'Port is not for the very young, the vain and the active. It is the comfort of age and the companion of the scholar and the philosopher. The particular qualities of British university scholarship – its alternations of mellow appreciation and acid criticism – may be plausibly derived from the habits of our senior common rooms.'
Evelyn Waugh,
Wine in Peace and War

'An old gourmet
who's grown somewhat stout,
Felt a twinge and much feared it was gout.
"If I drink now," he thought,
"Three whole bottles of port,
It surely will settle the doubt." '
Laurence Sterne, *Yorick*

'Is anything the matter with Mr Snodgrass, sir?' inquired Emily, with great anxiety. 'Nothing the matter, ma'am,' replied the stranger. 'Cricket dinner - glorious party - capital songs - old Port - claret - good - very good - wine, ma'am - wine.'
'It wasn't the wine,' murmured Mr Snodgrass, in a broken voice.
'It was the salmon.'
(Somehow or other, it never *is* the wine, in these cases.)
Charles Dickens
The Pickwick Papers
(1836-7),

'He has just had a basin of beautiful strong broth, sir,' replied Mrs Bedwin.
'Ugh!' said Mr Brownlow, with a slight shudder.
'A couple of glasses of Port wine would have done him a great deal more good.'
Charles Dickens, *Oliver Twist*

'When rectors drank Port Wine,
When no man talked of grace,
What jolly days were those!
Ah! then a parson's face
Displayed a parson's nose, –
A parson's nose of red,
Which gloriously did shine,
Supremely strong of head,
When rectors drank Port Wine...
Verses from *Punch*, 1870s

In a moment he'd taken a bottle of Port from among the sherry, beer and cider which filled half a shelf inside...Some of the writing on the label was in a Romance language, but not all. Just right: not too British, and not too foreign either. The cork came out with a festive, yule-tide pop which made him wish he had some nuts and raisins; he drank deeply. Some of the liquor coursed refreshingly down his chin and under his shirt-collar. The bottle had been about three-quarters full when he started, and was about three-quarters empty when he stopped. He thumped and clinked it back into position, wiped his mouth on the sideboard-runner, and, feeling really splendid, gained his bedroom without opposition.'
Kingsley Amis, *Lucky Jim*

'So that was it then, the Canon relieved after a fashion, pushed away his half-finished dessert and declined the offer of coffee from the senior curate. At the mention of Fransesca's name and the awful prospect of the Christmas dinner which he could not avoid, he instantly decided that instead of the glass of Port to which he would normally address himself, he would finish off the bottle which contained, in his humble estimation, at least three glasses. He felt it was his inalienable right in view of what he would have to suffer shortly as a consequence of parochial custom.'
John B Keane, *Voice of an Angel*

'Some great eccentrics broke every standard of accepted behaviour, making them famous in their lifetimes even though their underlying motivation remains mysterious. One such person was Jack Mytton one of the most notorious hellraisers of all time, whose life was understandably brief (1796-1834). Expelled from both Westminster School and Harrow for fighting, he gave away money and spent about half a million pounds on alcohol in seventeen years. Port was his favourite drink at a rate of five bottles a day, but at a pinch, *eau de cologne* or lavender water would do. His wardrobe contained 150 pairs of riding breeches, 700 pairs of boots, more than 1000 hats and nearly 3000 shirts .'
David Weeks and Jamie James, *Eccentricity*.

'But alas, there was one moment when disaster came from the master's habit of sharing all good things with the subject beast, for a horse named Sportsman dropped dead because John Mytton, out of the kindness of heart, had given him a bottle of mulled Port.'
Edith Sitwell, *English Eccentrics*.

Back to basics

The basic facts behind the making of Port have been simplified in this section, to provide both the expert and the amateur with an easy reference to the region, the wine making, and the serving of Port wine. The most common questions have been addressed and answered.

Port is a fortified wine grown and produced in the valley of the River Douro in northern Portugal. The wines are aged in the Port lodges (cellars) of Vila Nova de Gaia - across the river from the old town of Oporto. Port is a naturally rich and full wine, fruity and fiery in the case of Ruby Port, delicate and complex in the case of Tawny. It is the wine of kings, dukes and lords, enjoyed by everyone who tries it.

Douro Valley
- the demarcated region

Located in the North of Portugal, the demarcated region stretches from around 100 km east of Oporto towards the Spanish border. The area was the first delimited in 1755-6 by the Marquis de Pombal, and is the oldest demarcated wine-growing district in the world, and the only delimited area that can produce Port wine.

The area comprises 250,000 hectares of which only around 30,000 are under vine. The climatic conditions ranging from freezing cold to burning heat.

The Douro Valley is a patchwork of micro climates caused by the mountains and valleys which influence the way the different grape varieties produce each year. There are three major sub-regions: Upper Corgo, Lower Corgo and Douro Superior.

Port Wine

Port wine is made from grapes grown in the Douro Valley demarcated region.

The natural fermentation of the grapes (the process in which the grape sugar is converted to alcohol) is stopped through the addition of high proof brandy (neutral wine alcohol, 77% vol.) which maintains high residual natural sugar/sweetness. Port wine has 18-22 % alcohol by volume and around 100 gms of sugar per litre.

Port wine is protected under the "Denomination of Origin - Porto".

After an initial year of storage in the Douro Valley, the Port wine will mature in oak vats and casks at ageing lodges (cellars) in V. N. Gaia.

Port wine reaches a minimum average age of three years before being bottled and placed on the market. It is always a blend of similar yet distinctive wines that are put together to create a specific style decided on by the company which makes and ships the wine. All Port wine bottled at origin is registered and certified and bears the guarantee stamp of the Port Wine Institute.

> *"Wines that heaven knows when had sucked the fire of some forgotten sun and kept it through a hundred years of gloom."*

Blending

At the beginning, wines are concentrated in colour, with fresh fruit aromas (like fresh plums) and 'raw', unmarried alcohol intense in the nose; too young to be fully appreciated.

During the maturing period in storage, wines will gradually evolve from their primary characteristics: the intense ruby colour alters to lighter ruby or amber and the aromas evolve - they can reach from well-married alcohol and fresh fruits to well-balanced dried fruits and oak. Wines which initially show different potential will evolve in different ways. Similar wines stored in different storage containers (vats/casks) will also evolve in different ways. It can happen that a wine intended to be a Ruby alters too rapidly and it will end up as a Tawny.

Vintage Ports

Vintage Ports are exceptional wines from a single year, very intense and deep in colour, presenting an enormous concentration of fruity aromas. These wines are bottled two years after the harvest, without any treatment, and continue their maturation in the bottle over a period of 10-15 years.

Tightly sealed, they will evolve in the same way as great Bordeaux. During maturation natural sediments will form and the wines become more complex. The decision to declare a vintage is exclusive of each shipper and needs the approval of the Port Wine Institute. Vintage Port must have the potential for greatness on bottling, and the structure to keep vibrantly alive for decades.

These outstanding wines are a gift of nature, which is why there is rarely a universal declaration. If more than half the shippers declare a vintage in one year, that year is declared as vintage year for Port wine.

Single Quinta Vintage

A Single Quinta must produce enough outstanding wine in a single year to declare a vintage, but the odds are stacked overwhelmingly against this happening. The Port is made and matured in the same way as Vintage Port.

Storage

Vintage Port will mature in the bottle for 10 - 15 years or more. This unique wine must be kept laid down on its side so that the cork is kept in contact with the wine. This keeps it moist and tightly seals the wine from the air. During storage, Vintage Port will form natural sediments.

Serving

Vintage Port should be handled with care. Stand the bottle upright for at least 12 hours. Open with great care not to disturb the sediment and cloud the wine. The most traditional way (and probably the best either for old Ports as well as other old wines, such as Bordeaux) to open a bottle of Vintage Port is by 'tonging' the neck of the bottle. For this you need the proper equipment: iron tongs adapted to the neck of the bottle, source of heat (an open fire will do nicely) and some ice. Carefully apply the hot tongs to the neck of the bottle, allowing the heat to penetrate the glass, then rapidly remove the tongs and rub ice over the heated area. The thermic shock will produce a clean cut, leaving the bottle ready to decant.

Decanting

The slow and steady pouring of the Vintage Port into a decanter ensures that no sediment clouds the wine. This wine has been sealed away from air for decades, so it undergoes a shock when opened. As oxidisation begins, the wine will start to reveal its best qualities and reach its peak, just like any great wine. Vintage Port should not be kept open for long. Depending on the wine, the average recommendation is that it should be consumed within, at most, 24 hours of opening.

Storing Port Wine

In order to preserve the unique qualities of Port wine, it should be treated with care. The guide below illustrates the ideal storage conditions for each type of Port, and should be followed carefully.

- Constant temperature 10°- 20°C (50°- 68°F).
- Constant humidity around 60% rH.
- Shade/semi -darkness conditions, avoiding bright, intense natural or artificial light.
- Bottles sealed with straight corks (Vintages) should be stored in a horizontal position.
- Bottles sealed with stopper-type corks (all non-Vintage Ports) should be stored in a vertical position.
- All Sandeman Ports (except Vintages) are fully matured and bottled ready for drinking.
- The considered optimum storage period for Port wine (deluxe aged Tawnies and Vintage excluded) is 12 - 18 months.
- Vintage Ports are exceptional wines that mature in the bottle. Their storage period is unlimited, and they are best after a minimum of 10-15 years.

White Port is made from white grapes and can be sweet, medium sweet or dry. There are both young and old White Ports but the recent trend is for young, light, pale and fresh White Ports. These are usually served chilled as aperitifs or in long drinks, with a splash of tonic water ('Sandeman Splash').

Ruby Port is made from red grapes and has the characteristics of young wines. Rubies have intense, deep red colours, full, fresh, red fruit aromas and rich flavours. They are produced in the same way as all Ports and are kept in large oak vats to maintain their initial characteristics. Depending on their ageing potential, as each wine is different, Ruby Ports can be classified as Original (or Standard), as Reserve, or within the Special Categories ranges - i.e. Late Bottled Vintage (L.B.V.s), Vintage Port, Single Quinta Vintage Port.

Late Bottled Vintages are Ports of a single year of good quality that have been fully aged previous to bottling and are bottled between the fourth and the sixth year following the vintage. LBVs are ready to drink when bottled and should not require decanting.

Tawny Port is also made from red grapes and has the characteristics of aged, evolved wines. Tawnies present amber colours, aromas of dried fruits and spices and are very intense and complex in the mouth.
They are aged in small oak casks so that they evolve faster from primary characteristics and develop secondary colours, aromas and flavours.
As with the Rubies, Tawny Ports can also be classified in the Original (or Standard), Reserve, or the Special Categories ranges - Wines with Indication of Age (10, 20, 30, more than 40 years), and Wines with indication of Harvest Date (also called *'Colheitas'*).

Wines with indication of age, like the Sandeman 20-Year Old-Tawny, are a blend of different wines, which have aged together over 20 years and achieved a composition and balance to create the characteristics of a 20-Year-Old. The indicated age is not a mathematical average.

For further information, please contact
Ligia Marques, Sandeman, Oporto
Telephone: 351 2 370 6807 Facsimile: 351 2 370 6816

SANDEMAN RANGE OF PORT	OPTIMUM SHELF LIFE*/ OPEN BOTTLE LIFE**	SERVING SUGGESTIONS	
***ORIGINAL RICH RUBY (AGED 3 YRS) FOUNDER'S RESERVE (AGED 5 YRS) LATE BOTTLED VINTAGE (SEE HARVEST DATE)	**1 year after purchasing** Taste unaffected up to 1 month After 2 months: slight oxidation/loss of fruit; natural occurrence of cloudiness/sediment	Serve with chocolate desserts (mousse, bitter chocolate cakes), rich creamy cheeses (Camembert, Brie), and red fruit pies (plums, strawberries/berries) Red, juicy meats/ richly cooked fish. Very good for sauces.	R RUBY
****ORIGINAL FINE TAWNY (AGED 6 YRS) IMPERIAL AGED RESERVE TAWNY (AGED 8 YRS+)	**1 year after purchasing** Taste unaffected for up to 2 months After 3 months: some oxidation and loss of freshness; natural occurrence of cloudiness/sediment	Serve slightly chilled as an aperitif or accompanying some appetisers (blue cheese quiche, *vol-au-vents aux fruits de mer*). As a dessert wine serve with dried fruits and nuts, pies, cakes, apple pie, blue cheeses (Roquefort/Stilton/Bresse Bleu)	T TAWNY
ORIGINAL FINE WHITE (AGED 3 YRS)	**1 year after purchasing** Taste unaffected for up to 4 months After 4 months: some oxidation/loss of fruit (White Port will last better if kept in refrigerator)	Serve chilled as an aperitif or as a long drink such as the 'Sandeman Splash' – 50/50 Sandeman Original Fine White + Schweppes Tonic Water + ice + lemon. Superb for a summer night! As a dessert wine serve with vanilla ice cream, banana and passion fruit.	W WHITE
TAWNY 20 YEARS OLD TAWNY 30 YEARS OLD	**4 years after purchasing/ Unlimited** Taste unaffected up to 4 months Natural occurrence of cloudiness/sediment; some oxidation (decant if necessary)	Serve slightly chilled as an aperitif or accompanying some appetisers: (*foie gras,* Roquefort quiche). Serve at the end of the meal with blue cheeses, rich egg/almond cakes.	D DELUXE AGED TAWNY
VINTAGE PORT SINGLE QUINTA VINTAGE PORT	**Unlimited/Best after 10-16 years** Taste relatively unaffected up to 24 hours After 24 hours: strong oxidation/loss of fruit (decanting necessary)	After careful decanting let the Vintage breathe. Appreciate on its own or in the classic way: with Stilton cheese, nuts, figs.	V VINTAGE

(*) **Optimum shelf life** refers to the optimum period during which the wine remains at its best after bottling and coming to the shelf. Usually all wines are prepared bearing in mind they will face transport, storage and handling before arriving on the shelf.

(**) **Open bottle life** refers to the period of time during which the wine will keep its main characteristics, namely freshness.

(***) In some countries this wine is found as *Partners' Port, Old Invalid Port* or *Three Star Port*.

(****) In some countries this wine is found as *Five Star Port*

acknowle

OPORTO

The House of Sandeman
3 Largo Miguel Bombarda
4400 Vila Nova de Gaia
Portugal
Tel: 351 2 370 6807
Fax: 351 2 370 6816

LONDON

Davys Ale and Porthouses
Tel: 0181 858 6011

Alastair Little
136a Lancaster Road
London W11 1QU
Tel: 0171 243 2220

Anton Edelman
The Savoy
The Strand
London WC2 R OEU
Tel: 0171 836 4343
Fax: 0171 240 6060

Anna Hugo/192
192 Kensington Park Road
London W11 2ES
Tel: 0171 229 0482

Deborah Bosley
Gentle Jayes
Jo Warren

Bibliography:
The Guinness Drinking Companion,
Leslie Dunkling (1992, Guinness
Pubs.)
Food and Drink in Britain,
C. Anne Wilson (1973, Constable)

*Sandeman: Two Hundred Years of
Port and Sherry*, Ned Halley
(1990, Sandeman)

VENICE

Dr Natale Rusconi
Hotel Cipriani
Guidecca 10
30133 Venice
Tel: 41 520 7744
Fax: 41 520 3930

Count Carlo Maria Rocca

Victor & Marcella Hazan

ORIENT EXPRESS

Venice Simplon-Orient Expess Inc.
Sea Containers House
20 Upper Ground
London SE1 9PF
Tel: 0171 928 6000
Fax: 0171 620 1210

THE RIVIERA

Hotel Negresco
Restaurant Le Chantecler
37 Promenade des Anglais
06000 Nice, France
Tel: 93 88 39 51
Fax: 93 88 35 68

Hotel Martinez
73 Boulevard de la Croisette
06400 Cannes, France
Tel: 92 98 73 00
Fax: 93 39 67 82

Fondation Ephrussi de Rothschild
06230 Saint Jean Cap Ferrat, France
Tel: 93 01 33 09
Fax: 93 01 31 10

Hotel Carlton Inter-Continental
58, Boulevard de la Croisette
06400 Cannes, France
Tel: 93 68 91 68
Fax: 93 38 20 90

Hotel Juana
Avenue Gallice
La Pinède
06600 Antibes, France
Tel: 93 61 08 70
Fax: 93 61 76 60

Restaurant La Mère Germaine
7 Quai Courbet
06230 Villefranche-sur-Mer, France
Tel: 93 01 84 42
Fax: 93 76 94 28

Le Grand Hotel du Cap
Boulevard Général de Gaulle
06230 Saint Jean Cap Ferrat, France
Tel: 93 76 50 50
Fax: 93 76 04 52

Musée Picasso
Place Mariéjol
Château Grimaldi
06600 Antibes
Tel: 92 90 54 20
Fax: 92 90 54 21

Musée Matisse
164 Avenue des Arienes

06000 Nice, France
Tel: 93 81 08 08
Fax: 93 53 00 22

Hotel Le Saint Paul
86 Rue Grande
065760 Saint Paul de Vence, France
Tel: 93 32 65 25
Fax: 93 32 52 94

Chapelle du Rosaire
Avenue Henri Matisse
06140 Vence, France
Tel: 93 58 03 26

Le Moulin de Mougins
Quartier Notre Dame de Vie
06250 Mougins
Tel: 93 75 85 67
Fax: 93 90 15 15

Hotel du Cap Eden Roc
Boulevard JF Kennedy
06600 Antibes Juan les Pins
Tel: 93 61 39 01
Fax: 93 67 76 04

Hotel Splendido
13 Viale Baratta
16034 Portofino, Italy
Tel: 185 269551
Fax: 185 269614

Hotel Abela
223 Promenade des Anglais
06000, Nice, France
Tel: 93 37 17 17   Fax: 93 71 21 71

French Tourist Office

178 Piccadilly
London W1V OA1
Tel: 0891 244123

The French Riviera Tourist Board
55 Promenade des Anglais
06000 Nice
Tel: 93 37 78 78
Fax: 93 86 01 06

ANTWERP

Belgian Tourist Office
29 Princes Street
London W1R 7RG
Tel: 0891 887799
Fax: 0171 629 0454

Antwerp Tourist Board
Grote Markt 15
2000 Antwerpen 1
Tel: 03 232 01 03
Fax: 03 231 1937

SOUTH WEST IRELAND

Ballymaloe House,
Shanagarry, Midleton,
County Cork
Tel: 353 21 652 531
Fax: 353 21 652 021

Blue Haven Hotel
Kinsale,County Cork
Tel: 353 772 209
Fax: 353 774 268

Bantry House,
Bantry, County Cork
For accommodation

and information:
Tel: 353 27 050 047
Fax: 353 27 050 795

Moran's Oyster Cottage
The Weir
Kilcolgan
County Galway
Tel: 353 91 796 113/083
Fax: 353 91 796 503

Bibliography :
The Voice of An Angel by John B
Keane, Published by Mercier Press,
Cork, Ireland.

The Bodhran Makers
by John B. Keane,
Brandon Book Publishers Ltd.
Dingle, Kerry, Ireland

NEW YORK

Paramount
235 West 46th Street
NY, NY 10036
Tel: 212 764 5500
Fax: 212 354 5237

The Royalton
44 West 44th Street
NY, NY 10036
Tel: 212 869 4400
Fax: 212 869 8965

Gotham Bar and Grill
12 East 12th Street
NY, NY 10003
Tel: 212 620 4020